To Phylliss my dearest friend much love Ellen

Where I Come From

The Well Done Writers

Collected & Edited by Lori Thatcher

We Write Publications

Copyright © 2017 by Lori Thatcher and the individual members of The Well Done Writers.

All rights reserved. No part of this publication may be reproduced, distributed or transmitted in any form or by any means, including photocopying, recording, or other electronic or mechanical methods, without the prior written permission of the publisher, except in the case of brief quotations embodied in critical reviews and certain other noncommercial uses permitted by copyright law. For permission requests, write to the publisher, addressed "Attention: Permissions Coordinator," at the address below.

Lori Thatcher/We Write Publications
2800 N 6th St, Unit 1, PMB 185
St Augustine, FL 32084
www.welldonewriters.com

Book Layout ©2013 BookDesignTemplates.com

Ordering Information:
Quantity sales. Special discounts are available on quantity purchases by corporations, associations, and others. For details, contact the "Special Sales Department" at the address above.

Where I ComeFrom/ Lori Thatcher. —1st ed.
ISBN-9781539833314

Contents

Where I Come From 1

This Place - These People 25

It Happened Like This 59

Sounds, Light, Action 87

Tell Me 111

Memories of Millie Grant 135

ABOUT THE AUTHORS 139

*This Book is dedicated to the memory of Mildred Grant,
longtime member and cornerstone of The Well Done Writers,
who passed away in 2016.*

The original "Where I Come From" poem was written by George Ella Lyon, Kentucky poet laureate 2015-2016. The story of the poem and the writing prompt that grew out of it and which has traveled around the world and been used in schools and jails and at family reunions can be read on her website: georgeellalyon.com

Lori Thatcher originally brought the prompt to the members of The Well Done Writers Group. This book contains some of the writers' responses.

CHAPTER ONE

Where I Come From

Dolly Arsenault

I'm from the O'Hanlons and the Quills, who chanced leaving the Emerald Isle for the promise of America.

I'm from a Fifties childhood of Howdy Doody,
Little Lulu, paper dolls,
floating Popsicle sticks down rain-swollen gutters and capturing grasshoppers and fireflies in empty Hellman's jars.

I'm from listening to my father's bedtime stories
made up on the spot.

I'm from eating greasy fried clams at Christy's, followed by necking in cars with boys who reeked of Old Spice.

I'm from executing the Hully Gully with the precision of a Rockette.

I'm from multiple readings of life-changing books: *A Tree Grows in Brooklyn, Black like Me, To Kill a Mockingbird*.

I'm from music that clutched my soul: Tom Waite's husky,

plaintive songs; Queen's "Bohemian Rhapsody;" and Les Paul's acoustic rendition of "Starry, Starry, Night."

I'm from women ahead of their time: my mother, my aunt, and my sisters; they exemplified true femininity,

And I'm from such good men: my father, my brother, and my uncles. Their lives raised the bar on the two remarkable men I'd marry.

I'm from the bliss of holding my newborn daughter and watching my timid child turn into an amazing young woman with a strong voice.

I'm also from the grace of being present when my husband went from pain to peace. That grace freed me from my own fear of death. It was his final gift to me.

Janet Keyes

I'm from country-mouse territory where some folks had thinly veiled scorn for city folks who were afraid of a little manure, or who wondered if cows bite. I'm from places where the term "gentleman farmer" was more insult than compliment.

I'm from a family who spoke in embarrassingly odd phrases like "I don't know but what..."

I am from the family who never told me phrases like that came from Dickens, maybe because they did not know.

I'm from a time when poor folks were born at home, and babies were nursed, not bottle-fed.

I'm from the generation for whom electricity was a novelty to be used carefully and economically.

I'm from a lifetime of living in used old houses, and one new house. I'm from don't throw it out, just fix it up and make it useful again.

I'm from a one-room school where the teacher was conscientious but slightly cruel. I'm from a junior high school where many people were routinely crude and callous. I'm from a community college where no one was cruel, even to awkward misfits.

I'm from blackberry vines and bramble-damaged shirts and heavenly shortcakes. I'm from a childhood of trees to climb, wildflowers to pick, lightning bugs to chase, dusty barns with haylofts to jump in, multiple attics to explore, chores to do, brooks for wading, kittens and calves to cuddle, jack knives and homemade bows-and-arrows, and endless books to read.

I'm from years of laughter about a "key-poohey," based on the enraged demand of a frustrated toddler who could not say "clean spoon," but could doggedly make her needs known.

I'm from a time of belly laughs about a "beb dodcat" found in a story written by a dyslexic first-grader with a delightful imagination and a tendency to mix up "b's" and "d's."

I'm from birthdays shared with my older sister, whom I suspect imagines she heard me say on her fifth birthday, "I and you will share this birthday," a precursor to another conversation I overheard forty- three years later when my young son sat on his older sister's lap while she ate ice cream. "I and you will share this ice cream."

I'm from a family where gatherings feature the younger generation quoting pages of dialog from favorite old movies, and gales of laughter erupting when the mimicry is especially good.

I come from home-canned stew beef, home-grown and over-cooked vegetables, home-canned peaches, pears, and blackberries, pale pink spaghetti, mulberry pies and prune pies, and homemade root beer. I am from an adulthood of learning how not to cook like my mother. I am from greasy delicious Village pizzas, and low-fat delicious homemade pizzas.

I come from miles of Christmas memories: Opening gifts on Christmas Eve; Uncle Levi and Aunt Flossie coming for Christmas dinner; wreaths made of green construction paper leaves of cut-out tracings of small hands; small shepherds in old bathrobes and rag-strip belts, carrying homemade crooks; small angels with wire-coat-hanger-and Saran-wrap and silver rope garland wings and halos; little hand prints preserved in plaster of Paris; homemade Christmas cards; Christmas turkey-never-ham dinners; Christmas pageants and Cantatas.

I am from a full life of joys and sorrows, testing and triumphs, growing and learning, working, caring, loving.

I am from a time of denying, cursing, battling, struggling, coping, surrendering, and then embracing the sundown and twilight time of my life.

Estelle Cade

I'm from the granite bedrock
of icy Maine waters;
the pull of the sea, the push of the tides,
starfish and hermit crabs,
seaweed and sea gulls' cackle,
and sailing ships.

I'm from the soft hills of the lower Berkshires -
open pastures, mountain laurel and mayflowers.

Gardens full of ripening corn,
fields of onions and potatoes.

Cowbells ringing, murthers* of crows convening.

I'm from the city - trains running,
subways swooshing through,
the wind causing me
to grasp my mother's hand more tightly.
Stand back of the line - fear that mysterious third rail.
The eye of the train, red, glaring
as it approaches our stop.

I'm from a brook that babbles on -
bluets and violets waiting to be picked.
Blueberries and raspberries
and asparagus and rhubarb -
scenes from a country childhood.

I am from books and more books -
reading is fundamental.
Without a book or two in hand I am miserable.
And writing of course - if I cannot write
I am also miserable.

I am from cursive writing, table manners,
one telephone in the house.
One record player, one TV as the time went on,
and from families living cooperatively.

*Murther of crows - a variant of Middle English form - changed eventually to a murder of crows. More "poetic" they thought, than a flock of crows.

Ted Scott

I'm from Fox Lake Wisconsin, where you hardly see anything much. There's no airport, no train station. Not even a bus goes through these parts.

"But how do you get there?" you say. You can get a train to Milwaukee, then take a bus to Beaver Dam, which is ten miles south of Fox Lake. Then you walk or hitchhike from there, or maybe there's a bus to Ripon, which would get you to five miles west of Fox Lake and a shorter walk. But we did the hitchhike. That was fun, a lot faster than walking, and cheaper than the route through Ripon.

That trip led to our summer of fun, sweating, and riding on trucks for me, and fun factory work for Sidney and Harry, who left at the end of pea season, while I stayed on for the corn.

Fox Lake is the kind of a town where the weather is so hot and sticky that they give you a thick, black rubber raincoat to wear in the fields. At the end of the season it turns up missing and they take 30 bucks from your pay.

It's the kind of town where the morning starts so early that at noon you feel like you ought to be done. But then comes the evening, which sometimes wraps around midnight and you wonder when morning will come.

Fox Lake is the kind of town where you don't meet any people except to work without talking, or to pay an outrageous bill for your rent. It's the kind of town where you feel like a second class citizen. You'd like to speak with your fellow workers in the field, but their language is a kind of Creole that they didn't teach at your school. Besides, they work so hard that they don't even speak to each other. They all come from Jamaica on a three year contract to harvest America's crops.

They taught me to work as hard and fast as I could.

Fox Lake is the kind of town where you want the flies to go away, the rain to fall, the day to be over at midnight, and the awful canteen droning of "You've gotta have heart" to change to "Mr. Sandman" or "It's my Party."

Fox Lake is the kind of town where you count the days in the season, hoping to make it to the end, and if you do, you're proud.

But that was all 61 years ago. Now Green Giant's in Mexico, and I don't know where Fox Lake is.

Alice Thomas

slowly   a woman bends her knees - her back

issues a new generation   brings it forth

ideas and language – friends parks – dandelions and fountains

cupcakes and college

she cannot see the blue future or grey graves

but slowly   geography apparent

she rocks   remains silent   and waves

Janice Lepore

Referred to as the Midwest, where the sky starts at ground level, South Dakota is known for its Black Hills and the famous sculpture of four presidential faces, a mesmerizing look at history.

Having grown up in the far southeastern corner of the state back in 1930, I was a Massachusetts resident long before I actually saw the historic Black Hills.

For whatever reason, I don't recall the adults telling us children stories of their growing up—or even stories of their adult years. Maybe it had something to do with the depression years and the work they had to accomplish day in and day out.

We lived on a farm a dozen miles from anywhere and the dust blew constantly. I recall the farm buildings as grey even though I know they were painted.

I grew up the eldest of the first three of my parents' fourteen children, and I managed to be responsible for all the situations we three got ourselves into. We'd crawl up a half door at the barn to get on a bareback horse to ride around the big yard. It was great fun until the day my moccasin caught on a board by the corner of the barn. The board hit the horse, and we went sailing past the water tank and into the animal yard. My mother had been on the phone cancelling a piano lesson and witnessed everything. I don't recall ever riding the horses again.

Another time we got into trouble, we walked to Grandma's house a mile or so from our home. We had to walk past great fields of huge sunflowers. My uncle caught us in the act and he knew we had no permission to travel those back roads. He appeared out of nowhere from behind the sunflowers, broke off one flower and used that sunflower to whack us all the way home. Now sunflowers are considered beautiful and useful, but in South Dakota back then they were just big weeds.

After we were sent off to St. Joseph's boarding school, we no longer had our farm experiences. It was a whole new life.

Cathey Boschen

I am from St. Louis
The Midwest, Yugoslavia, and the South

I am from Faye and John,
    Bessie and John Sr.

I am from snickerdoodles and strudel,
    The accordion and a sofa bed.

I am from family gatherings on holidays
 cigar smoke, spaghetti and lime Jello salad

from Monopoly, Clue and Old Maid

I am from the enchantment of old movies;
Gene Kelly and Scarlet O'Hara

I am from polkas and waltzes, the Beatles and the Twist

I am from Slovania with the dream of America
I am from Arkansas and the myth of the South

I am from the world of learning and imagination
from honesty and hard work

I am from poverty and want; the land of unfulfilled dreams
I am from journeys of courage and hope

I am from Larry and Jon
from the love of dear relatives and friends,

I am from the universe and this creation
from the sun that shines, the earth that sings

I am from the heart of God, the gift of love,
I am from all of those who came before me.

Lori Thatcher

I'm from sand, the Montague sand plains which sprung from the delta into ancient Lake Hitchcock, and which surrounded my grandfather's farm. Sometimes I thought I would never be able to scrub all of that sand out of my hair and ears.

I'm from blue jar Noxema on my mother's bureau and coal black Iodex slathered on every cut.

I'm recently from Austria on Nellie's side, from Stanislaw Kurtyka and Agnes Slazak and old-country peasant farmers.

On Robert Haskin's side, from American pioneers, railroad men, engineers, stokers, and conductors on the Boston and Maine.

I'm from skinny telephone books, Forest 2770 and party lines where the neighbors listened in.

I'm from black and white and only three channels, all with snow.

From Ed Sullivan, from The Beatles "She Loves You" to The Animals "House of the Rising Sun."

I'm from hand pumps, a lone kitchen faucet, and the last working outhouse in Western Massachusetts.

I'm from bareback and horse sweat and haul your own water

when the well runs dry.

I'm from whiskey bottles lovingly filled with boiling water, wrapped in a sock to warm the blankets.

I'm from Uncle Charlie fishing at the farm pond and throwing back pumpkin seed, Mrs. Kosis who bought me *Lost Pony* in fourth grade, and the entire *Black Stallion* series borrowed from the library one at a time.

I'm from the Twenty Third Psalm and the Hail Mary. From "Don't tell anyone we don't go to church" to "Thank you God, thank you car" after every trip to town.

I'm from don't want and don't deserve and you can't possibly succeed. From warped views of a world where everyone is out to get you, from held grudges and bitter family feuds and "Why would anyone help us?"

But also from a mom who pointed out the clouds, treasured the smell of swamp pink blossoms, and taught me to notice things.

I'm from empty photo albums and only one faded baby picture of me before the school photos started. I'm from fat ass and talk too much and you'd be pretty if you just lost a little weight.

I'm from the sticks and the farm, from want and longing, but not from the poorhouse.

I'm from the same place where lots of people are from, precious places to remember and stark places to rise above.

Lettice Randall

Where did I come from
Oh, so long ago.
From Exeter born and
from there I did go

to Shelburne and Leyden
I did get around.

Where did I come from?
Was I lost and then found?
Where was I from on
that day long ago?
Playing with stuffed teddys
and kids I did know.

Sitting in classrooms
And there were quite a few.
Making friends in each town
On my journey there through.
So, where did I come from
And when did I arrive?

I came in '46 and
I'm still quite alive.
Now I know where I came from
And it makes me quite glad.
The truth of it all
I came from my mom and my dad!

Marty Glaser

I am from a lost world of prayer by ancient Rabbis reading Torah under candlelight.

I am from a Russian Balalaika which played Lithuanian and Russian melodies I sadly remember from my younger days.

I am from reading the Harvard Classics which broadened my rural attitude and made me into a worldly cosmopolitan man.

I am from a thirteen year old General Class Amateur Radio Operator who talked to the world with Morse code and tin cans.

I am from homemade chicken soup, the best cure for the common cold, told to me over and over by my Bubbe Jenny, Aunt Bertha and my mother.

I am from fasting on Yom Kippur to atone for my mistakes and be worthy to God and myself.

I am from my Zayde Isaac's Samovar, which he carried on his back as he left his home, Ponedel, Lithuania, for forever.

I am from a stickel for a nickel (a dry, hard, round piece of salami) served from a barrel at Weintraub's Delicatessen on Water Street in Worcester, Ma.

I am from my Aunt Bertha's tsimmes (cooked carrots and prunes together) which was so sweet and tender, served hot at her Passover Seder.

I am from my lilac bushes that smelled so fragrant and from the luscious pears I stole off Bubbe Jenny's pear tree when I saw she wasn't standing guard.

I am from the aroma of the large Challah wafting through the air from Bubbe's cooking stove which also held two small Challahs for Jerry and me.

I am from my father's dental lab which created the silver to fill the teeth that had cavities.

I am from the musty smell of dust and oil on my baseball glove after thirteen years of inactivity.

I am from a Bar Mitzvah boy who is counted as a tenth man for a minion for Kaddish (memorial prayer).

I am from the smell of illegally caught pickerel when the game warden told me to throw them back into Sportsman's Pond.

I am from a lawn which smells sweet from a recent mowing.

I am from qvelling (looking with love and pride) at my first granddaughter, Olivia, smiling up at me, and my second grand daughter, Addy, wanting me to chase her around our house.

I am from a dream life where you wake up at sixty-nine and see your grown sons having families of their own.

I am from the love of my parents, Aunt Bertha, and Bubbe Jenny, as we gave love to David and Seth, our sons.

I am from those two sons who are my heroes and my inspirations.

I am from a world of my parents who married during the Great Depression and taught me Glaser's Laws of Economics.

I am from Eastern European Ashkenazi Jews who came as Jewish immigrants in 1920 to build a life in the United States and continued their cherished traditions without fear.

I am from a 5,778 year history of Jewish survival, which was dependent on Torah, great minds, and love of justice.

Luci Adams

I am from pinafore aprons,

from Arm & Hammer and Boraxo.

I am from a huge iron and tin monster bellowing out heat, smelling warmth.

I am from hedges and boulders

worn smooth and shiny from many rains.

I am from big gatherings at Thanksgiving,

from people with Roman noses and high cheekbones.

I am from Bill and Madeline Adams

from Baxters, Munsons, and Schimmel/Schmidts.

I am from the plowing of fields and ministering to people's souls and carpentering…

From Black Forest and landed gentry.

I am from pro-test-ants, and earth-based philosophies - Native American, Celtic, and Germanic roots.

I'm from "The Midst of the River" city; Daughters of the Mayflower…and

Mill River flood.

I am from home canned vegetables, fruits, jams, and mac and cheese, meatloaf and mashed potatoes.

I am from a sister who liked to eat mustard by the spoonful, an uncle who built caskets.

I am from an uncle who left home in 1900 to drive stagecoach from Worthington to Northampton.

I am from a great uncle who fought in the Civil War, returning to his roots in the hill towns of western MA.

I am from a large duffle bag on the top shelf in the closet - faces from the past; now a small shoe box stored in a foot stool – some transferred to a huge collage of more-present faces, now just memories as they, too, are in the past.…………

Whispers from the past, old lace and full length dresses, stove-pipe hats, horses and old Tin Lizzies are what I am from.

Gone are those days. So grateful to have the picture memories -

spanning three centuries.

I am from many times and many places

Timeless, eternal, joyous.

Noreen O'Brien

I am from a wringer washing machine;
from a triple decker corner house
and a neighboring ballfield.

I am from scrubbed floors
and Pine Sol and furniture polish.

I am from a weeping willow tree,
whose draping branches, hung so low they touched the ground
and hid my shame,
leaving me unseen.

I am from books and board games;
from Jack and Iva.

I am from sarcasm and generosity,
and from a potty mouth and a flash of anger.

I am from a guilt-ridden Catholic faith.

I am from a hard-drinking, professional boxer and a sublime
beauty, who was once a roller derby queen.

From a spaghetti-sauce-Wednesday supper,
and a Sunday dinner of corned beef and cabbage

—which included the week's only dessert.

From a grandfather lost at sea;
and a beloved uncle who died young,

struck down by a hit and run driver.

I am from these moments of poverty and riches,
of gifts and losses, of cleanliness and beatings,
of anger and deep love.

Sherry Payne Kohler

Austin Texas, University Town
My Home #1

There was a lap, warm and soft.
My mother was an artist.
My father was a poet.

The financial Crash
and the Great Depression
were four years old.

My mother washed my diapers outside
in a big round metal tub.
Her sheets arrived at our door
wrapped in brown paper, tied with purple ribbon.

Our living room was a center for talk.
There were chairs, mattresses, pillows and music.
Beethoven, Vivaldi, Schubert, and Lead Belly in person.

The talk was of art, music, and psychology
while I got to play "Find the thimble
among the pillows, the friends, and all the sounds

I am thinking today that the 1930s

are the premonition unacknowledged 'til now
although vividly laid out in the paintings
by Wood, Benton, Sheeler, Jones, Hogue & others.

Alex Houge painted "Erosion #2: Mother Earth Laid Bare."
The Industrial Revolution was upon us
hubris, invention, plunder & consumption.

Unto now, we are poisoning, polluting, destroying, exterminating
every drop of water, every breath of air, every bit of soil,
every flora, fauna, fungi and microbe.

Our artists and seers are among us still.
It's up to all of us to find the treasure of Empathy
among and within our Community of Life.

Ellen Blanchette

When people ask me where I'm from, I frequently answer Brooklyn, because that's the place I think of as home. If they press me, because they don't hear a Brooklyn accent, I'll add that I grew up in Philadelphia. Now I live in Massachusetts, which means I've lived in three of the thirteen original states involved in the founding of our nation. The degree of history surrounding our lives in these places was part of my upbringing and influenced the way I think of our country. Somehow the intent of those great men who lived in those times and wrote those documents that are the basis of our democracy, looms large in my imagination as I contemplate what it was like to be them in those times of revolution and change. What kind of courage did it take to do all the things they did? How did they manage to be so brilliant and far sighted in their thinking? It dwarfs anything we do today, where we seem to be dominated by fear in so many aspects of our lives.

In Philadelphia we live with Ben Franklin staring down at us from on high, his statue on top of city hall. In New York City there are lots of statues but none that call out to you to live up to the standard they have set like old Ben does. He was signatory to the Declaration of Independence and member of the Continental Congress, brilliant leader, author, inventor, scientist, our ambassador to France during the revolution. Who could live up to his achievements today?

I grew up in a small neighborhood in West Philadelphia made up of primarily first generation Jewish Americans and their families. We were a block from the city line, a fancy community of big stone homes with wide lawns just on the other side. For a while, there were trees along the road blocking our view of that community but someone built a shopping center along City Line Avenue with lots of little stores, a fancy chocolate store and a very large parking lot. Not that we didn't walk back there before it was built, but once mobile, on bicycles, that parking lot surrounding the mall gave us an invitation for exploring we hadn't considered before.

The neighborhood itself was just a few blocks long, mostly attached homes with tiny slanted gardens in front and with wide porches connecting our outdoor activities. As kids, we sat out in the summer, played cards, hop scotch, and jacks. Our parents sat on lawn chairs and talked. We were a tight knit community in some ways but without any strong center that drew us together. My mother taught school and some of the other teachers lived in the neighborhood. She and my dad had friends to go with to concerts at the Academy of Music on Broad Street. I went to the children's concerts there on Saturdays with my mother sometimes and to the Settlement Music School for years of ballet classes. Mom and I had a routine. Saturday was our day together, and we often met my Aunt Marion for lunch after my ballet class

I loved the Philadelphia Art Museum and the Main

Library, and spent many hours of my youth there. This part of the city is a beautiful place, especially when the gardens fill with flowering trees and fountains are surrounded by flowers. Yet, socially, I felt stifled and isolated. I had good friends in the little neighborhood I grew up in, but school was a different story. The kids all seemed richer than we were, better dressed, and a little snobby. Cliques were part of high school. I never quite got what the girls were giggling about, never understood the rapid chatter of a dozen teenage girls all talking at once. I would stand in the choir room watching and listening and wondering what they were doing. At least I had the choir room, a place where I knew I belonged and felt appreciated, as we all were, for our musicianship and vocal skills. That made us friends without anything more expected of us. In high school, it was the one place I could be with the African American kids. Even though they were half the student population, they were not in my classes. I can't say why, except that it seemed the Jewish kids took the academic courses and the African American students were encouraged to take the commercial courses so they could work when they graduated. While it was probably a mostly economic choice, there surely was some racial bias in the counselors' minds as they guided young wonderful African American men and women away from academic pursuits, encouraging them to become typists and office clerks instead of teachers and doctors and scientists.

In New York City, the city hall in lower Manhattan is a grand building that spreads out over several blocks with arches you can drive through. There the heroes are mayors like Fiorello and La Guardia, and governors like Mario Cuomo and certain senators like Robert Kennedy and Jacob Javitz. Mostly they get plaques and streets named after them. For a statue you need to be dead a long time and probably some kind of war hero. For me, however, the heroes are strong women like Bella Abzug and the ghosts of our revolution in the '60s, civil rights leaders, women who stood up and fought for women's rights, people whose words carry us forward.

Whatever else we did in that great city, the most powerful efforts were the marches and demonstrations against the war in Vietnam. I think of warm days in Central Park, people young and old but so many of us young, newly aware, passionate about a cause, and dressed in flowing multicolor shirts and dresses, tie-dyed T-shirts, young women and men with long hair a protest of sorts against neat and tidy. We wanted to be free of constraints that kept us in rigid positions in life, workers in shirt and tie, husband wife parent dressed for the PTA or the kid's softball team. Could we be more? Could we let our hair grow, dress in jeans, wildly colored shirts and dresses and spend our lives on the beach or on the road? Could we be free to explore what else life could offer? Questions our generation is still asking. Can we do it differently? Could we find a better way?

Now I live in Greenfield, and this part of Massachusetts seems the place where many people landed after the world of protest and social change morphed into daily lives of jobs, responsibility, and a turn back, however we dressed, to the lives our parents had led. Only our lives were frequently torn apart by forces beyond our control, economic, political, social change that drove families apart, abandoned secure middle class lives and left workers struggling to get back what they had lost. Today it feels like the power brokers have succeeded in returning to the world they had in the 1920s when rich bankers and corporate moguls ruled the day and workers had no rights at all. Smart, powerful men with a plan spent the last 40 years tearing down what we all worked so hard to build up. And yet, in this small town, I find opportunity I never had before, to follow creative dreams with art and music that were once my passion but were put aside for devotion to family and plain ordinary survival.

It is spring as I write this. The flowers have been blooming all around us and you don't need people to create pretty spaces because everyone contributes their own small space to the larger picture. I find an openness and willingness to nurture, and share creative opportunities with others that in New York City is rarely found. People go to New York to follow their dreams and end up waiting tables and working as part time receptionists, free to take time for auditions, and spend years doing that before they give up, go back to school to get degrees in business or economics, glad to get that full time job with benefits, and face reality that their dreams cannot come true. Plus they prefer to eat and have a roof over their heads.

Here, at this time in my life, I feel a freedom to follow those dreams and devote my life to taking whatever path calls to me, and even now at this age, perhaps achieve some small amount of success as I would define that for myself. To sing a song, create a painting, write a book, offer some bit of thought to the world that is valuable, this would please me greatly.

Esther Johnson

Almost daily, I awoke to different smells wafting through the house, but a constant smell in my childhood home was coffee. Strong Swedish coffee is not the watered down stuff Americans drink. My husband described it as being strong enough "that you can stand a spoon upright in it." It was never bitter like Starbucks and Seattle's Best.

Now to get back to those wonderful smells I woke up to. One day it would be yeast breads either from Swedish Limpa, a sweet rye or Vetebröd, Swedish cardamom coffee bread. The next day it might be kallops, a Swedish beef dish of stewed meat seasoned with bay leaves, whole allspice, and whole white pepper served with boiled or mashed potatoes and vegetables.

I grew up in the City, on a bus line, in a two-family. My parents were immigrants and so were our neighbors. None of them could afford their own homes, so they created the condominiums of their day. Two families bought a house together. My father and his brother bought our two-family (the Andersons). On our left two Italian brothers bought the house (the Salvatores).On our right an Austrian brother and sister bought the house (the Holzmans). On their right were the Polish (the Petorskis). It gave all of them the American dream.

The same builder built all those tenements in the early 1920s. Only one family did not have a formal living room.

My brother grew up there, with the neighbor's children. Because I was a lot younger, when I was young I was the only child in any of these households. Their grandchildren came to visit occasionally. My friend Debbie lived further down the street. Her father grew up with my brother. Her family bought out the downstairs owner so they owned the entire two-family. They had a three-bedroom, and their cramped tenement housed five children, Grandma and Mom and Dad. Their upstairs front porch and dining room were used as bedrooms also.

My friends are like America, a melting pot. When I was a teen and allowed to leave my street in search of friends, my best friends became other first generation Americans, a Pole, a German, an Italian, and an Armenian. I have found that I relate to first generation Americans better than other Americans who have been here for generations unless they truly understand how precious freedom and voting are.

My father died when I was nine. My mom's part-time job became our main source of income. My mother and two of her sisters-in-law had a catering business. Today people doing this job are private chefs. They went to peoples' homes and prepared and served the appetizers, dinners, and desserts as well as serving the cocktails. By the time I was 13, I worked with them when someone called in sick. Mom brought home leftovers from many of these events. It gave me a chance to try foods I never would have tasted otherwise.

Debbie's dad owned Dan-Dee Donuts in Agawam. Once they were able to write legibly, Debbie and Lee each night wrote up the delivery slips for the donuts for the next day. This is how they earned their allowance. As the children got older, the delivery slip job moved down to younger children. When the girls came home from school, they would go in to work with their dad Friday afternoon and Saturday afternoon to help make donuts. Alternatively, on Saturday and Sunday the girls sold donuts in Agawam. In that house, they never ate donuts.

We were from working families. We had to help, and that was how we earned money. Money wasn't just handed to children. The same was true for my other friends. My grandchildren expect to get money each week "just because" not because they earn it. They're not from the same place that I am.

CHAPTER TWO

This Place - These People

Good From Evil Intent by Mildred Grant

My brother was looking for a fight! He tried to engage my sister's attention by poking her in the back enough times and hard enough to warrant a full swing slap across his face. Angrier than ever, he tried to pick on me, but Mom caught him.

"Outside! No more picking on the girls! Go find someone your own size," Mom scolded. "Don't go far. We're in for a shower."

"Hm-m-m, my own size. That's it!" His face still smarting and now hot with rage, Chet stormed out of the house. Sneaked past Mr. Burt's farm. Dad might wonder where he was going if he happened to be looking. Up the next right hand turn and quite a bit further to where the big Rumrill family lived. The family wasn't just large in numbers, 10 children, but they were all large in size for their ages.

"Georgie! I'll tackle Georgie." Suddenly, right in front of him, in the middle of the road stood Georgie. Hoping to gain an advantage, Chet kicked a large stone, hitting his adversary on his right cheekbone. With a roar, Georgie came barreling straight at him. Instinctively, Chet sidestepped and brought clenched fists down on Georgie's neck and back.

Mom's warning about a rain storm when Chet left home came true, but the bolt of lightning that preceded the rain came just as Chet's fists came down on Georgie's neck and back. The bolt shattered a nearby, old growth chestnut tree, top to bottom. Georgie's scream of terror rivaled the decibels created by the following ear splitting clap of thunder. Though he didn't scream as Georgie had, Chet was badly frightened by the brilliant flash of pink lightning, the smell of brimstone, burning hair, and the shattered, smoking tree.

Georgie wasn't moving! Now Chet was very scared. As he reached out to see what was wrong, the heavens opened the floodgates of a cloudburst. Georgie's clothes began to steam, giving his whole body an eerie phosphorescence that flickered, then glowed.

Chester's wildly beating heart felt about to burst.

Over the snapping of chain lightning and the continuous crashes of thunder, Chet, nearly in tears, shouted, "Georgie! Georgie! Wake up!"

As Chet started to reach out to try to shake Georgie awake, a deep voice said, "Don't! Don't touch him!"

Chet, squatting down beside the stricken boy, sank back on his heels in order to take in the huge man that loomed over them.

"Oh, Mr. Rumrill, the lightning—," Chet began.

"I know what happened. I saw and felt the whole thing from my front porch," shouted Mr. Rumrill. He went on, "Boy, pick up that branch, no, the bigger one over there, if you can handle it. Now, drag it over here and put it next to Georgie."

Forgetting his own trauma by following Mr. Rumrill's directions gave Chet a temporary sense of stability that enabled him to do as he was told.

For the first time, Chet noticed the long stick Mr. Rumrill was holding.

"With this stick I'm going to try to roll Georgie over onto the green branches you just put beside him," he said.

Chet was puzzled, so he asked, "Can't we just pick him up?"

Anger sparked in Mr. Rumrill's eyes as he snapped, "I would if I could!"

Seeing Chet's fearful backward step, he explained in a calmer voice, "I've been very sick and don't even have the strength to help my own son."

Chet asked, as he picked up a sturdy, straight stick and offered to help move Georgie, "What do you want me to do?"

Mr. Rumrill glanced about the rain-shrouded scene in helpless frustration. Even the youngest Rumrills were away with their mother. The older ones were all away working. Georgie had been left at home to care for his Dad—now in reverse positions.

Drawing in a quick, decisive breath, Mr. Rumrill directed Chet to stand across from him, with Georgie and the large tree limb from the shattered chestnut tree, between them.

"Now take your stick and push the branches as close as you can get them to Georgie and the main part of the limb."

Chet found his assigned task to be very difficult to accomplish, but, by standing on the water soaked branches as he drew them toward the main limb, they would stay in place. How to make them stay that way would be a problem once he stepped off of them. Mr. Rumrill solved the problem by coming around the low stack of branches, taking Chet's stick and jamming it into the softened ground close up to the outer edge of the low pile of branches.

Back in his original position Mr. Rumrill, with Chet's help rolled Georgie over onto the leafy pallet. Now Georgie's weight held the wet and pliable branches in place fairly well.

Georgie was beginning to moan weakly and there was

slight movement in his fingers and bare toes. His eyebrows, eyelashes, and hair around his face were singed to a dirty white.

Seeing Chet's shocked expression Mr. Rumrill remarked, "If the loss of his hair is the only result of this experience, he's a very lucky boy. Now, please grab the end of the limb and see if you can help me drag him up to the house."

As man and boy reached for the torn branch, Chet noticed Mr. Rumrill's hand was very unsteady and he wondered if he should even try, but the big man jammed his makeshift walking stick into the soft ground and together, they began to drag Georgie up the sharp incline to the house. Nearly there, Mr. Rumrill was wheezing hard with every breath and step. Chet had to pull harder as his partner began to cough as well as wheeze. Exhausted, man and boy melted down to the top step of the porch.

Mr. Rumrill was trying to get something from his shirt pocket just as Georgie raised up on one elbow, reaching desperately toward his father. Seeing Chester, he gestured, frantically for Chet to help his dad. "Pill," he gasped. "Pocket!"

Chet, still breathing heavily himself, reached into the pocket of Mr. Rumrill's red plaid flannel shirt and found a small tube shaped metal container. Through gestures and a few barely understandable words, Chet finally understood that he should give the man a pill from the metal tube.

"How?" Chet asked. "Water?"

Over the still very noisy storm, and with great difficulty, Georgie shouted, "No! Dad, open your mouth! When he does, slip the pill under his tongue."

Chet did as he was told. In seconds Mr. Rumrill's breathing became more normal, but Georgie, though awake, lapsed into a deep lethargy.

The storm had moved on, though the sky was still split with brilliant shafts of lightening, and thunder rumbled ominously in the distance.

For a few minutes just the patter of rain broke the silence.

Chester was beginning to realize he was in a situation well over his head. Looking at Mr. Rumrill and Georgie, he understood they both needed the care of a doctor.

Down on the main road, further haying for the rest of the day being out of the question, Mr. Burt had just asked Chet's father to find out if there was any storm damage on his land up the hill.

The next sound Chet heard was that of approaching horses and cart. Chet sprang to his feet, but his overtaxed legs wouldn't hold him upright. His dad had stopped the team at the storm blasted chestnut tree. In desperation he called out, "Dad, Dad, Up here! Help!"

Urging the team of horses up the now muddy incline, Chet's dad wondered out loud, "Chester, what in the blue blazes are you doing way off up here and soaking wet! Your mother must be frantic!"

"Please, can I explain later? Mr. Rumrill is sick and Georgie needs help," Chet cried. His son being his first concern, and finding him in reasonably good shape, Chet's dad gave the rest of the scene a quick assessment. Though Mr. Rumrill was taller and heavier, Chet's dad had him resting in a porch chair in no time with an additional pill under his tongue. Georgie was a different matter, but Chet's dad made a quick decision based on previous training, to send for the doctor as soon as possible. As he spread a blanket from one of the porch chairs over a now shivering Georgie, Chet's dad explained his decisions to Mr. Rumrill who nodded, weakly, in agreement, saying, "Go easy on your boy. Whatever his reason was for coming up here—well, he saved our lives."

Grandpa and Superman by Lori Thatcher

Legs pumping the bicycle pedals, I made the two miles in short time. I didn't have a minute to waste. A dime smoldered in this nine-year-old's pocket.

I stopped at Bartley's store first because it sat right on the big curve as you entered the village. The new issue had to be out by now, and if Bartley's didn't have it, I could check Sontag's or Buckmaster's, the other two mom and pop stores that served Montague Center in the 1950s.

But he was there, behind Batman and next to my second favorite, Wonder Woman. The cover of the Superman comic book was brilliant with his bright blues and reds, and in the background lurked his bald-headed nemeses, Lex Luther.

I didn't thumb through the copy. I knew Mr. Bartley would look over my shoulder to make sure I wasn't trying to read it without paying. I hurriedly handed over the dime: Grandpa's dime.

My family had lived with my grandfather until I was seven while they saved up money and my father built a house. Then we lived a short way up the road from Grandpa, in a small ranch house on a piece of land carved out of his acreage.

Once we moved, and following some family quarrel I didn't understand at all, we didn't visit Grandpa any more. Ma said we couldn't go inside his house because other relatives objected. But he asked me to stop when I bicycled past and Ma never said I couldn't wait at the road and talk to him while he sat on his front porch.

I paused on the edge of the hardtop and balanced on my bike. Grandpa always said, "You growing like a corn stalk," and asked me how school was going. I offered answers minimal at best. I was shy around adults and I didn't feel very comfortable with Grandpa. When we had lived with him, he talked little and seemed to require quiet just when my younger brother Bobby and I got the loudest. Even though we lived in a separate part of the big farmhouse, Ma cautioned, "Pipe down. If you disturb your grandfather, he'll get mad and give you a whipping."

Years later I recognized that my mother occasionally coupled her own demands with warnings of consequences imposed by others.

I never remembered Grandpa mad. Still, the dusky, wiry little man concerned me. He didn't look or speak like any of the rest of my family. Ma said his skin was dark because he had spent so much time outdoors tending his farm and gardens, and that under his shirt, his chest and upper arms were as creamy white as a dove. Even after he hadn't farmed for years, his skin continued to resemble the cherry wood of his crook-handled cane.

I lingered at the road and he stayed on the porch. After a minute or two, when conversation on the usual subjects petered out, we settled into silence, with him rocking in his rocking chair—fast and slow and fast again—and me straddling my bike and scuffing a foot in the dirt at the edge of the road. Even though I was impatient, I was reluctant to ask for what I wanted.

Sufficient time had to pass before he slowly got up, stretched, and wiped his brow with a folded handkerchief. He stepped down the two stairs and shuffled across the patch of weedy lawn with his cane barely skinning the ground. From his old leather change purse, he extracted a dime and held it out to me.

"Go buy book."

That's how he spoke, not "a book," just "book," and it sounded more like he was saying "pook." Ma said he was from the old country and didn't learn English until he was a teenager. She told me that many immigrants kept their accents no matter how long they lived in America.

I yelled thanks to Grandpa over my shoulder, and sped off single-mindedly.

Usually I saw a few kids from my elementary school riding bikes along the way to town, but most weren't friends and I didn't want to stop to talk anyway. I wanted the Man of Steel.

When I whizzed past Grandpa's house on the way home, I pulled out the comic and held it up while barely slowing. He'd smile and say something like, "Good. You go read."

I hurried home, hiding the comic under my shirt so Bobby wouldn't see it until I was ready to share. Then I secreted myself away to devour every word.

Just looking at the cover started a fluttering in my stomach. I couldn't wait to plunge into the landscape of courageous heroes. I could picture myself fearless and daring, strong as Wonder Woman, invulnerable as Superman.

After a couple of reads, I charged out the door and dashed down the hill behind our house. I imagined I might take flight at any second and yell loud enough to create hurricane winds. If I were Superman, I'd never dread walking into the cafeteria at lunch time, and if I were a proper Amazon like Wonder Woman, I could just pick up any kids who made fun of me at school, hoist them over my head and toss them in the manure pile. What better role model could a fainthearted little girl have?

A while ago, as I drove through Montague Center, I thought of one: Grandpa.

It had been fifty years since I was that scared little girl and I scarce recognized that Grandpa was the real Superman in my young life. He hung on and refused to let me go. He fashioned for me a bit of space in the midst of whirlwind family battles and buffered the forces of bitterness and petty feuds that surrounded us. Sounds like a real superhero to me.

And We Were Singing by Estelle Cade

Yes, there we were, all thirty of us on the risers with our sparkling director in front, dressed in elegant performance costume and singing with our usual skill and enthusiasm. We had been hired to entertain an audience of senior citizens at a gala luncheon in their honor.

And there was our audience. (You should know that performers look over their audience, reading them if you will, to present a program that will be just for them, even as an audience looks at the performers.) So, right near our risers was a table of well-dressed ladies, smiling at us and at each other, nodding their heads, mouthing some of the words—or maybe even trying to sing along a bit. They were wonderful. At one table, a brave couple even got up to dance a bit. We applauded them!

A few tables over, another group, all men (and quite elderly), was having a conversation about something, sports perhaps, and all mostly deaf it seemed, because as some of our livelier pieces grew a bit louder, so did their conversation. It became a kind of competition and we front-row people tried hard not to laugh as one gentleman in particular seemed to glare at us as though we were interfering with their conversation.

Then farther over in this rather large hall, there was yet another group - The Stone Faced Folk. Whether we sang a gentle ballad, a tune from a familiar musical or even our patriotic medley–which the older men especially always truly responded to—their expressions never changed. We thought some had even fallen asleep at some point in the afternoon.

It is very difficult to perform for what seems an unresponsive audience anywhere, but in this case, trying not to laugh kept our smile muscles right in place the entire time.

We ended our performance with appreciative applause

from those who had listened. And as for the others—we decided that those folks had already been embalmed but just hadn't lain down yet. Too funny! Some of us still mention that afternoon as we reminisce about other days, other moments together, and laugh once again.

Arriving- a New Beginning by Janet Keyes

It was September 15, a Sunday. I was moving to the nurses' residence of the Franklin County Public Hospital to start my nurse's training. I was scared. New things always scared me. Would I like the other girls? More importantly, would they like me? Would I be the smartest? Did that really matter?

I found my room, I think with the help of an older student. The room was small, but there was space enough for the bed, the bureau, the desk and chair, the closet door, and the sink. The bedspread and curtains were sturdy, institutional, and a dull salmon-pink color. I made a mental note to get a pair of real curtains and a bed cover I could like. There was room in the closet for the salmon-pink stuff to be neatly folded and out of sight.

I went back downstairs to the large parlor, where other girls were also entering. We were a small class, only fourteen girls. There was a bubbly dark haired girl, a merry looking blond, a cute redhead who seemed to be friends with an equally cute brunette, a sturdy and stern looking girl, an older girl who struck me as sophisticated, a pretty girl from Turners Falls, a stylish blue eyed and black haired Irish looking girl, a girl who looked even more terrified than I felt, a beautiful tall girl, a short and friendly girl, a short and cute blond girl, and others. My head was filled with first impressions and some confusion.

It was late afternoon and the kind older student, whose

name was Deanna, invited me to come over to the cafeteria and have supper with her. I gratefully accepted the invitation and felt more grown up than I should have. I have no idea what I ate. I remember only that as we were leaving, my classmates were all coming in. My heart sunk, as I realized I should have stayed with my own class. I was all alone now. Within the first twenty-four hours, I would learn that by leaving my classmates, I managed to miss a significant orientation speech and some special instructions, laying the groundwork for me to suffer some embarrassment. Back in the residence, I went to my room and did my unpacking. The queasy feeling in my stomach was not related to the food I had eaten.

My thoughts kept turning to the date I had enjoyed the previous evening with a guy I really liked. His name was Allan, and I hoped he would call me again for a second date. He was so nice, but at that point it would have been impossible for me to imagine we would be married in three years.

As the evening wore on, I found myself in the room of the bubbly brunette, who was earnestly saying, "I hope our class can all be friends. I don't want us to be broken up into little cliques, like those girls in the class ahead of us." I was not sure how she knew the lifestyle of the second-year girls, but I shared her hope and optimism. Our new life was beginning.

My Grandfather's Clock by Cathey Boschen

Up in our attic sits my grandfather's clock, broken in many pieces. When I was a little girl it sat in his house on an old wooden table in the bedroom. I remember the rhythmic ticking sound it made when I lay there in bed at night. The whole clock was about 18 inches tall. There was wooden scroll work around the face at the top and at the base, and in the middle was a rectangular glass case that held the pendulum and mechanisms for winding it.

I brought that clock with me when I drove from St. Louis to Massachusetts. At that time it was basically intact. I'm not really sure why I wanted it, but at the time it seemed important to keep it. My mother had moved to a smaller house and she was getting rid of so many things. I was afraid she would throw it out. It was just an old clock, but it was an important reminder to me of my grandfather and the times we spent at his place in Illinois.

As a little girl, I was crazy about my grandfather. As his only grandchild, I shared a special relationship with him. I followed him everywhere and we were constant companions. We often walked together in the woods and around the lake near his house. Anything he cooked, I ate. I remember getting up early in the morning with him. It would be very cold and he had a wood stove for cooking. When the oven was hot he'd open up the door and I'd rest my feet on the end of it to get warm. I loved sitting there all cozy and snug, watching him make breakfast. Another memory I have of my grandfather was that he loved to give me little shots of Rock and Rye whiskey, which had all this fruit in the bottom of it. I used to drink it down quickly in one large gulp. It tasted horrible and my mother soon put an end to it but it was fun to see him laugh when I drank it. It was our own little joke.

I was six years old when my grandfather died, on June 28th, my mother's birthday. At that time he had lived with us for a while. He had been very sick with gangrene and had lost a leg to it. I remember little of the funeral, but I do remember being at the cemetery at the gravesite. As we were leaving the grave, my father collapsed and the men around him had to carry him back to the car. It made a strong impression on my young mind.

Growing up we spent a lot of time at Grandfather's house, on weekends and vacations. Every time we went we always stopped at the cemetery first and my father made sure the grave site was nicely maintained. There were peonies there which bloomed every spring and every year Dad planted geraniums on Memorial Day.

Over the years I've kept that clock stored wherever I lived. I didn't pack it well enough to withstand the moves and over time it started to fall apart. It's in so many pieces now I don't know if it can be repaired. But I keep it anyway, along with the two large pictures that hung in his bedroom, one of my grandmother, who died when my father was little, and the other of my great grandparents from Yugoslavia. Except for old photos, these are the only tangible things I have of my grandfather's.

Whenever I go to St. Louis to visit my brother and sister we always go over to Illinois to see my grandfather's place. We stop at the cemetery first and check on the grave, often leaving potted geraniums. Then we go and visit where his house once stood. There are so many memories from long ago. Even though he died when I was very young, I remember my grandfather through loving eyes. His clock helps me to hold onto his memory.

Becoming a Villager by Dolly Arsenault

This was my family's reaction the day we told them Al had been accepted as a grad student at the University of Massachusetts.

"You'll be living in a village?" my older sister said. "There are still villages in Massachusetts?"

"In Western Mass there are," I said. "In fact, this village is one of, like, four in the Town of Montague."

"Don't worry," my husband added with a laugh. "It's not like we're—heaven forbid!—moving to a hamlet!"

"Why can't you stay in Boston for graduate school?" my

brother asked in his pragmatic way.

"There's only one reason we're moving," Al said. "Professor Wolfe teaches at U. Mass. I want to study under him."

"What is it you're studying again?" This came from my youngest sister. She'd been told many times he was going for his Ph.D. in philosophy but she never remembered. "I think you should just stay here," she said. "Just study under someone else."

As it would turn out, we would have been better served if we had stayed in Boston. But Al and I were full of youthful exuberance and naively imagined a golden future.

We'd had a tip from a friend of a friend that a cheap apartment was available in a place called Millers Falls. While it was a half-hour drive from U. Mass, it was also half the rent of a place nearer the University. Money would be tight: for the first year, we would only have what I could earn as a secretary. After that, Al would qualify for a teaching assistantship which came with a $2,000 stipend. So, trusting he would indeed get a TA and that we could live anywhere for a year, we rented the Millers Falls apartment.

We took off at dawn on an early August day in 1971. Most of the drive was on highways and was excruciatingly boring. However, when we reached the town of Erving, I saw things of interest. The first was an old farm house on Route 2 that had a weathered sign reading: "Annie's Apron's."

Wow! Some women still wore aprons. I'd never even owned one.

A little further up Route 2 was my next surprise, a working paper mill. It was still early in the morning and workers were straggling through the doors into the 19th century brick building. Almost all of the men were swinging metal lunch boxes while the women seemed to prefer paper bags.

"No one looks happy," I said to Al with a shudder. "This could be a scene out of Dickens, or a painting by Brueghel. Hard to believe such an old building is still operating."

"Where did you think paper came from?" He shook his head. "You've never worked in a factory like I did. You're used to cushy, clean office jobs." He shrugged. "It's a different kind of life here. Not a lot of jobs. You take what's available."

My next culture shock happened a few days later. I had wrapped our breakables in towels and curtains which were now wrinkled. Some were permanent press so I could forego ironing if I popped them in the wash. Curtains wouldn't do much to alleviate the dreariness of our second-floor walk-up apartment but they couldn't hurt. So, off to the laundromat I went.

We lived in the center of town and the laundry, drugstore, grocery store and library were within walking distance. I dumped several pairs of curtains in a washing machine. While they were sloshing, I walked to the library. By chance it was one of the weekdays it was open. It was a tiny space with few books, but the librarian, a pleasant, middle-aged woman, helped me choose some best sellers and offered to get what I wanted from other libraries. I thanked her and carried my selections back to the laundromat.

By then the curtains were washed and I shoved them in the dryer. As I did, a woman came in wheeling a baby carriage without a baby. Instead it held a heap of dirty clothes. That didn't strike me as odd; indeed it seemed a practical transport solution. What did strike me as odd was that the young woman had her hair in curlers. In public! I hadn't seen that in at least a decade. Then, as I waited for my wash to dry, more and more women, of all ages, came in with curlers.

For the next few weeks I frantically sought work. I went to the local hospital first, believing it would be a cinch to get hired there. After all, I'd been a secretary at Boston University Medical Center. Surely they would fall over themselves to take me on. But no; it seemed they could do without my services. So too could Greenfield Tap and Die and a few other larger employers whose names I've forgotten.

We were down to our last $300 when I finally got a job: ironically in the office of the very paper mill we'd passed on Route 2. I was almost immediately made Supervisor of the Steno Department and oversaw all typing tasks. Later I was instructed on using the IBM Magnetic Card machine and trained my five-girl staff in this computerized way of processing words. As a supervisor, I was paid five cents more an hour. I mockingly moaned to Al that I would have paid the company that extra $2.00 a week to be relieved of resolving the petty squabbles among my young typists.

I enjoyed the five years I worked at the mill. The office had about forty employees, many of them under thirty. Consequently, we partied a lot and became close.

My office friends were a welcome relief from that year's batch of Ph.D. candidates in the Philosophy Department. For the most part, the grad students were uptight, fiercely competitive and humorless souls who slavishly curried favor with the department head and their respective dissertation advisors. Al and I welcomed the respite of bowling or attending a simple pot-luck party with my fun-loving crew.

I've forgotten most of Al's fellow grad students, but more than 40 years later, I fondly recall all my office mates.

My Town- Greenfield   by Janet Keyes

Greenfield is the kind of town where you can see an increasing diversity of races and cultures. In places like grocery stores and the hospital, where no ethnicity can avoid being from time to time, one overhears a variety of languages. Perhaps the most active church in town is now the Muldovan Baptist Church.

Greenfield is the kind of town where many parents work together to maintain youth sports programs. The Lunt baseball fields and the Murphy Park softball fields are busy most evenings all spring and summer. The Greenfield tennis courts on Davis Street and next to Beacon Field are well-maintained by the town and often in use. All through the cold months the town ice rink is busy with ice hockey and figure skating. The YMCA hosts basketball and gymnastics programs. All these, plus dance schools, martial arts academies, and other venues, provide wholesome and interesting alternatives to sedentary activities like video games and endless texting.

Unfortunately, some good youth activities are in great decline. No longer are there places for roller skating or bowling, which used to be very popular. No longer is there a skateboard park, because the last one closed after some miscreants committed acts of vandalism in the area. One of the most obvious areas of decline is the Greenfield swimming pool which for years was a favorite gathering place for children, teens, and families. An influx of out-of-town hooligans and drug dealers caused the town to seek ways to control the pool area population. As a result, the entire park was isolated by an imposing and non-welcoming black iron fence, and all users had to pay hefty fees to enter. Now in the hottest days of summer, there may be only about two dozen cars there. Most days the playground stands sparsely used, and the town studiously avoids any possibility of locating a nice, accessible skateboard park in the northern half of this cold and sterile place.

Greenfield is the kind of town where half the people live in the past and the other half live in ignorance of the past. The YMCA of our childhoods is now buried under the immenseness of the modern replacement building. The library of our past of course no longer has familiar card catalogs or a quiet room for reading and research. There are just lots of computers guarded by swivel chairs stripped of their wheels, so that no one under six feet tall can sit and work at a computer for more than five minutes before acquiring a sore back and a stiff neck. Greenfield is the sort of town where half the people give directions in terms of references to places that no longer exist, such as "next door to where Don Lorenz Buick used to be" or "behind the old Friendly's restaurant." The other half of the people don't know or care much about where anything is or was.

Greenfield is a place physically bound by hills on the west, north, and east, and a valley to the south. It is defined by Poet's Seat Tower on the east, and Greenfield Community College and the old Long View Tower on the west. In the north end is the Pumping Station Bridge, and downtown has the Energy Park where the old railroad station used to be. In the south end is the beautiful Wiley-Russell dam on the Green River, and the shiny new brook trout sculpture celebrating both the river and some of the manufacturing history of the town. This pleasant, protected valley has gentler and milder weather than most of the surrounding hill towns.

Greenfield is a place of poetry, music, art, theater, history, pizza parlors, small trendy restaurants, small boutiques, historical buildings, an imposing new transportation center, large egos, and even larger differences of opinion about a possible "big box" retail store. Greenfield is a good place to live.

My Mother's Hands by Noreen O'Brien

The sound of a metal file brushed against a fingernail meant it was Sunday evening and Walt Disney was on. Dad, remote in hand, would be in his chair, dead center in front of the television. Mum, filing her nails, sat on one end of the couch, manicure tools on the seat next to her, and us five kids on the floor, sitting in a semi-circle in front of the television.

My mother had elegant, small hands, with a ring size of four-and-a-half. She took great care of them, typically with daily moisturizing and then her weekly manicure. Her nails were polished most of the time—nothing fancy or bold—rather a soft, subtle shell pink or a clear varnish, nails filed to a softly rounded point. Even her cuticles were manicured. Those small, delicate hands, beautiful as they were, were also weapons, the source of many beatings, most often given to me, perhaps because I was the oldest of the five children.

I vividly remember the very day—the very moment—I understood something about those beatings and my mother. I was twelve years old and working on my homework, sitting on the edge of my bed in front of a TV stand—remember those? I can't recall a time we didn't have these mini-tables, though they were never used to eat in front of the television, rather only for things like our homework or to hold Mum's curlers while she did or undid her hair.

On this particular day, I remember my mother was in my brothers' bedroom, yelling at them about something or other. It went on and on and on. I snapped, although I was trying very hard to hold it in. I don't remember if I raised my voice, or if I left my seat at the edge of my bed, but I do remember saying that I could not concentrate on my homework for all the screaming. I know I asked how I was supposed to do well in school, as was expected of me, if I was unable to do my studying in peace and quiet.

I can still feel the stillness that ensued.

I sat quietly crying. Waiting. And sure enough, it came. She approached me from behind my right shoulder, grabbed my long hair, and yanked me to my feet. "What did you say to me?"

I tried to explain that I only wanted to do my homework and I couldn't for all the noise. She grabbed my arm, swinging me so that my back was to the wall and she was standing on one of my feet so I couldn't get away from her. I'm not sure if I cried during those moments. I do know that I tried to stand tall and take the beating while looking at her full in the face. And that's when I saw the telltale look that forever changed my view of my mother.

I could see it in her eyes, written all over her face. She hated herself with every strike of her beautiful hand against my face, head, arm, back, whatever area of my body she could reach. And when contact was made to my body, she hated herself a bit more, didn't know what to do to stop from striking again, felt frustration, and hit me again. I thought she was going to kill me that day.

Mum and I never spoke of any of these goings on. In fact, over the years, when I would try to broach the topic, she denied she'd ever laid a hand on me. It took many a year for me to face up to her treatment of me and her denials. I had times when I would dry heave at the thought that I had passed through her birth canal, or that I had suckled on her breast as a newborn.

But you know, over the years I'd written so much about my childhood, my mother's inability to acknowledge what she'd done to us, me in particular, wrote so many "unsent" letters to both her and my father, I finally got a grip on things and recognized that I was looking to her for approval that I would never receive. This summer, at around the 21st anniversary of her death, I found myself writing about her yet again, but this time was different. Something I never once viewed as a possibility occurred. I discovered that not only did I love my mother; I recognized that I was *in* love with her.

I wrote Mum yet another letter that day, knowing she would never read it, but hoping she would know that I am so very sorry that I hadn't reached this place while she was alive, that I never had a chance to say that I forgive her and that I love her. Perhaps most importantly, I never had the opportunity to feel it and mean it during her lifetime. I want her to know and to feel my love for her. And that my hands may be curled and deformed from this arthritis, and I may not use a metal file or paint my nails with polish, but I still see her hands in mine when I do my manicure every Sunday evening.

Leaving Home by Marty Glaser

I left home many times. The first time I left home was when I went to a Boy Scout camp called Wiyaka. I spent the week learning how to tie knots, identify poison ivy and poison sumac by its respective leaves, make a fire and cook a meal, and make a shelter from trees to sleep outside. The most interesting thing I learned was how to bring a canoe to shore when it was filled with water. This took a long time paddling with all my strength. It was fun to be away from home for a while.

The second time I left home was when I was accepted as a boarding student at Worcester Academy during the years from 1960 to1965, which was far better than double sessions in Athol. I did go home for Thanksgiving, Christmas, and summer vacations but it was only to visit.

The third time I left Athol was when my folks thought I should go to Boston University of Basic Studies. This was in the fall of 1965. I think they wanted me to go to BU because Jerry was just across the Charles River if I needed academic help. They liked to take drives and visit us, and might have thought I needed more encouragement than Jerry. I lived in a dorm throughout my college years.

After two years, I decided to transfer to Emerson College and study to be an elementary school teacher and study Spanish. Don't ask me why. I have no idea!

I had to transfer to another college because BU College of

Basics Studies was only a two year program. You could transfer into the regular University or transfer elsewhere. Because I transferred to Emerson, my local draft board told me that my status would be changed to 1A. I explained to the draft board that I would complete my college education in two years. They did not believe me and changed my classification twice in two years. My brother Jerry was a scientist and therefore deferred from the draft.

I was concerned that I would be taken into the military before I finished my bachelor's degree, and I wanted to be around to receive my diploma, so I signed up with the National Guard.

I graduated from Emerson in August of 1969. When my parents and I returned home from my graduation, a jeep was waiting to take me into the military service. I showed them my 1-D card which meant I was a National Guard soldier. They left quite angrily.

When I got a job teaching fifth grade at the Ditson Schooling Billerica, I moved into a rooming house owned by Mrs. Medora Sanden, a French Canadian and a fantastic cook. I started the school year in September. On December 5, 1969, I received a letter from the President of the United States. The words struck fear in my heart. "Greetings from the President of the United States, blah, blah until the end of the letter which said," You will Report to Fort Jackson, South Carolina."

I had to immediately notify my principal and then Paul Hefernan, the school superintendent. He said to me, "If I knew you were a National Guardsman, I never would have hired you!" I left his office feeling lower than whale manure.

I took a plane to Columbia, South Carolina, and got on the bus which took all the new recruits to Fort Jackson. The bus stopped on a company street near lots of streets with WWII barracks. The drill instructor (DI), with the Smoky the bear hat, got on the bus and said, "You best all be off this bus in five seconds" I was trampled, bloodied and helpless.

After sixteen weeks of Army training. I returned to Billerica. I couldn't get my job back until September. I was pretty bummed. I talked to my father. He was very wise and asked me three questions.

The first question was, "What would Babe Ruth do when he struck out?"

I said, "He would get back up to hit again."

The second question was, "What would Ted Williams do if he struck out?"

"Dad," I said, "he never strikes out."

"But what if he did?" my father asked.

"I guess he would get up to bat and try again."

The third question came as fast as the other two: "What would Joe DiMaggio do if he struck out?"

I said," Get back up and bat again."

My father let the lesson of my three great baseball heroes sink into my brain. Then he said, "You only got to bat once. You have two more at bats to become a teacher, don't you?" He was right.

Leaving by Ted Scott

I'll never forget that bright fall day with the oak leaves and acorns littering our driveway and our daughter posed in front of that tiny black Ford Festiva we'd given her two years earlier. The last of the under $5000 new cars, which with its giant clam shell hat, held all of her camping gear and some of ours.

I half wished she was taking a boyfriend, even one I hated might have been better than this. Alone, all alone, for a trip to who knows where? She had reminded us that three years earlier, she spent two months alone on the road in Europe. That after the eight weeks at a small school on a Greek island with her college roommate from U Mass.

"Yes, but that was Europe," my wife complained. "America is much worse, much more dangerous."

I remembered that trip also, and the week that she hadn't called. Somehow my wife made it through all five stages of Kubler-Ross in one week. I was almost surprised that she was still sane when we finally got that long awaited call. It turned out there just weren't any phones in Italy. My wife had been strengthened by that experience. She was less worried now. She had even made arrangements for a private 800 number that could be called free from any phone in the country. I was more worried, partly because of my own experience thirty-some years earlier when I took a similar trip and it ended badly.

Two days earlier she'd had a job, a room in our big house, her own car and TV, and what seemed to be a fairly stable situation. She didn't have a boyfriend, but she'd had those before and I knew she could find one easily enough when she was ready. In fact some of her old boyfriends were still around and one or two still called, hoping she would take them back.

When she came home early from work that day, we wondered if something was wrong. She had only been working at that human resources place two months, just since she graduated. She'd been appointed Human Rights Officer only a week earlier. I didn't know exactly what that meant, but she seemed to be excited about it. She didn't talk much about the job. We knew the place was some kind of halfway house. But the smile of joy on her face that day was enough for us to wait for her story.

"They fired me," she said, "because I took the job seriously. As Human Rights Officer, I was supposed to represent the clients, and I did, and they fired me."

"But why?" I asked.

"The clients needed to smoke, and I could see that they

really did need to smoke, and some of the bosses smoked. There wasn't really any reason for the clients not to be allowed that simple pleasure. I just made their case for them."

"Is that all?" I was beginning to see both sides of this, but I'd never thought of either of my kids as lawyers.

"Well, it was when I suggested we take it up with the ACLU that they got nasty. They reminded me that I was still on probation for another month, so they could fire me without cause. That's what they did. They told me to take my things and leave. I got a check for two weeks' pay and I don't have to go back."

"Is that why you're so happy?"

"Yes. I didn't much like that job anyway, and now I've got enough money to follow my dream."

"Which is?"

"I want to go on a road trip. I've nearly always wanted to do that, especially since Europe, and now I've got a car and some money. With my savings, I've got almost a thousand dollars. I'd like to leave day after tomorrow." She paused, "I didn't mean to shock you, and I just hadn't expected it to happen so soon. You did something like that once, I think."

I decided not to remind her that I had been younger, less experienced, without a car, almost no money, and was not even halfway through college, but I was a male. I could see that none of those arguments would help. I could see that this was the time, if there ever was such a time. Well prepared, compared to me at least, no children, marriage, or other major ties. No reason not to go, except for me and my wife, and the fact that she was our daughter. I just wished we could see it that way.

She said she'd be gone for a year.

Insight or Idea by David Allen Bryant

I had an idea that I thought would make things better for me back around 1982. After thinking about it for a year or more, I decided to move to L.A. It would be a permanent move. I had a few relatives who had moved there in the early 1960s. I got my plane ticket and in a few days, I was on my way from Bradley Airport in Connecticut to New York where I would make the change to a larger plane, and six hours later arrive at L.A.

As I stepped off the Pan Am Plane, I saw my aunt and her daughter there to greet me. My aunt said she wanted to show me the vicinity so we drove to Hollywood, up Wilshire Blvd, and to Beverly Hills.

Once we arrived at their home, I got settled in. After about two weeks, things started to change. We lived maybe four blocks from downtown Los Angeles and twenty minutes from Hollywood. I wanted to get into school and, after checking out a couple of different ones, decided to go to Barbazon School of Modeling. The person in charge at that time was a tall, slim, young woman named Lena, a model-type with a very dark tan, who persuaded me to enroll. She was a very loving and caring person and I sought to build a serious relationship with her. As time went on, she called every day, frequently asking me when I was going to enroll.

Eventually, I could tell that it wasn't working out with my relatives, namely my aunt and uncle. I had not made any intimate friends since I got to L.A., so I had to take up my aunt and uncle on their suggestion to leave. They said that their daughter, my cousin who had been born retarded, had wanted to move out and get an apartment with me, but she would always say and do unexpected things, so that wouldn't work out.

I wanted to stay in L.A., but with such a short-term notice,

I had no time to get situated. They said I had to go back to Massachusetts, and took me to the bus station.

It was a long, long ride back. I left at Tuesday 7:00 p.m. and arrived in New York at the Port Authority Friday at 9:00 a.m. Still, it was a beautiful experience in California. After a while, I called Barbazon Modeling School and they said Lena no longer worked there.

So I took it all with a grain of salt. You live and you learn.

Breakthrough by Alice Thomas

we hold the book
two hands

then   raise our eyes
brim the highest edge

and escort
the sentence of it all

The People I Came From by Esther Johnson

I was born when my father was 53 years old. God did not give him many years to spend with me. I was nine when he died. Three years later, my mother remarried, a man 20 years her senior. My stepfather was not a substitute for my father. Having had no children, he had no idea what it meant to have a teenager in the house. We were cordial to each other but that was the extent of our contact.

    When I was 19, a tragedy in our family gave me a new "father". A car driving down State Street in Springfield hit and killed my cousin Karen. Karen and I had been close friends. After that happened, it became second nature to ask Uncle Dick to take me to Father/Daughter Banquets instead of my stepfather. My stepfather and I never went to any joint events. My aunt and uncle invited me to their family events where my mother and Eric, my stepfather, were not invited. I had become one of their children.

    When my husband and I bought a house, it was on the same street as my uncle. He taught us how to make the quality renovations our house required. We lived in that house for twelve years. We saw each other every day and our children knew them as aunt and uncle. My aunt was my mother's younger sister, being 16 years younger. Her children were my age.

    My husband's job moved to Gardner, MA and so we moved to Greenfield. While they lived in Springfield, we continued to see my aunt and uncle a lot, but once they moved to Montgomery, MA our visits were less frequent. As my Aunt Eleanor's health became worse, Uncle Dick and I began talking weekly. My oldest cousin, Anthony, in California began calling more often discussing both his mother's and father's health issues because he knew I was speaking with his dad. None of my aunt and uncle's children were local. One was in California, one in Florida and one on Cape Cod. I was the closest. I was always the closest of the nieces and nephews and still am.

Homage to The Moon and The Sun by Sherry Payne Kohler

It's always personal
That tree, that ocean
That loved one
Worth my very breath
Like the new-hatched turtle
Scrambling out of the sand nest
Hurtling across to the sea
No guarantee
Someone hatched me
They did their best
It's up to me

Silence of the Stones by Mildred Grant

    The immense granite blocks forming the foundations for both my great-grandfathers' barns were quarried in North Adams or Vermont. They were brought up out of North Adams and over the mountain by block and tackle. Stone boats drawn by teams of oxen took them over land to the prepared foundation sites. Again, block and tackle was used to lower them into place, an expensive operation both in money and physical effort. Those blocks, could they talk, would spin some interesting yarns and whisper deep secrets but, unfortunately, I haven't figured out a means of communication with them. Perhaps the following story, based on known facts, would be one of the secrets they would tell. It happened at my Great-Grandfather David Sherman's farm.

    A week had passed since a neighbor, Mr. Goldthwaite's burial. There were no apparent plans for the future of Mrs.

Goldthwaite and nothing left after selling the small farm to care for her. Her son, who was unaccounted for, would ordinarily have stepped up to the task, but no one knew where he was.

Mr. Goldthwaite's largest debts were owed to David Sherman, my great-grandfather, who was paid in full when the house and land were sold. No one knew what was going to happen to Mrs. Goldthwaite, now homeless and having to vacate the property as soon as possible.

David and his neighbors felt a moral responsibility to step in and help Mrs. Goldthwaite in her now desperate situation. David offered to help his neighbors build a small, one room cabin on his land, just beyond his barn. A shallow, 8'x8' foot hole was dug and equal sized field-stones were placed in the corners. These were topped with four large notched tree trunks spanning the front, back and sides. The walls were made of boards gleaned from the several sawmills operating on Dunbar Brook. The door and only window were salvaged from David's former home that had been destroyed by fire.

Though his new home was quite large, his big family of ten took up every inch with no room to take in Mrs. Goldthwaite.

Weathertight? No, but the roof was solid. In those days it was the barn that was best protected from the elements. After all, the animals provided some of the farmer's food, power for farm machinery, and most of their income. David's own house could have used a great deal of "chinking", Indian style. A process of stuffing every void in the house walls with new moss every fall.

Mrs. Goldthwaite lived there for three seasons, but two reasons for a drastic change reared their ugly heads. A winter of extreme, bitter cold and snow depths that necessitated tunneling from David's home to the barn in order to take care of the animals. After the present storm, trying to look after Mrs. Goldthwaite was a real problem until David's father-in-law, Alvin Tower, came by on the main road driving a team of large, sturdy horses hitched to a huge log snow roller, and noticed that the drive to David and Maryette's wasn't open. Urging his team forward, the horses plunged into snow up to their bellies. In summer, Alvin admired his son-in-law's choice of land for building his new house but, in this kind of weather, even getting to the house was going to be a challenge.

When laying out the drive, David had clear cut a curving forty foot wide swath from the main road to the house lot. He built stone walls on each side of the drive the full, winding, gradual length up to the house lot and barn area.

As Alvin neared the house, he heard a window open and his daughter's voice calling to him.

"Father, Father, please try to swing wide to the east of the barn. David is trying to get to Mrs. Goldthwaite with our horses and sleigh."

Alvin waved, letting Maryette know he understood her directions. What he didn't understand was why he should feel obligated to help rescue the woman. Rumor had it that she meant more to David than was considered appropriate for a married man already with a wife and several children. As Alvin pondered the situation, words his father had said to him many years ago, flashed into his head. "Never judge anyone until you have walked a day in their shoes!"

Having rounded the east-side of David's barn, Alvin could see David making slow progress with horses and sleigh toward the tiny cabin. Smoke coming from the chimney assured both men that the Widow Goldthwaite had recently fed her source of warmth.

Together, the men stamped out a rough path to the cabin door and knocked. The door opened slowly, revealing a figure dressed in every piece of clothing she owned.

Alvin took charge of the situation by saying, "Mrs. Goldthwaite, please bring your necessary items and come to stay at my home, at least until other living arrangements can be made."

Seeing David standing behind his father-in-law, Mrs. Goldthwaite said, "David, please don't think of me as ungrateful in any way, but I must consider moving on with my life.

You, Maryette, all of your family have been more than good to me. Until recently, some of our neighbors have been more than kind and generous. Oh, yes, I've heard the rumors, totally unfounded. I'm old enough to be David's mother." As she spoke, Mrs. Goldthwaite was gathering her most essential possessions into a basket. She went on speaking: "I am feeling much stronger than I did after my husband's death and quite equal to mounting an extensive search for my son." She concluded as she stepped through the door of the little cabin. As though to memorize the scene, she turned in a complete circle, nodded her head and climbed into the sleigh the two men had just turned around.

Alvin, with David's help, unhitched the mighty beasts from the snow roller, re-harnessing them to the other side of the log, ready to go back the way they had come, further compacting the snow and making the passage of the sleigh much easier.

"Mamma, girls, come look and see what Papa and Grandpa are doing," cried Elsie.

Maryette and her girls crowded around the window to see David driving Alvin's horses and the rumbling snow roller back toward the main road while Alvin drove the sleigh, runners squeaking, over the perfectly packed snow.

This is only one of the secrets those beautiful granite blocks might tell. Would careful listening produce a story or a secret from the same kind of blocks forming the foundation of my Great-Grandfather Stafford's barn?

Retirement by Janice Lepore

Now that Frank is retired, he sleeps in a recliner, on and off, all day long, while supposedly watching television game shows, sports, news, or whatever catches his fancy. How he can go to bed at midnight and sleep soundly after all his recliner snoozies, I'll never understand. He would make a great advertisement for "Lazy Boy" or whatever brand is their competitor.

Frank truly seems to be content as an armchair observer to life. A lifetime of piecework in an old factory building on a rotating shift schedule could be the reason. That type of work environment could affect people differently—some probably want to be foot loose and fancy free, where others, like Frank, enjoy a comfortable routine. We all agree that he has earned whatever kind of retirement he wants.

Whenever anyone questions his lifestyle, Frank will sit up straight, lean forward, look them in the eye and ask earnestly, "Is everything all right?" And the conversation will drift off in another direction. Of course he realizes and enjoys the fact that his brothers-in-law are just a wee bit envious. It's even a family joke with the nephews as to whom Frank will leave his beloved recliner in his will.

Retirement means different things to different people and we've come to the conclusion that dozing in a recliner is an art form that Frank has mastered and we are all happy for him.

Angelore by Alice Thomas

you asked about angels:
do they fly   play ball
order fried chicken
are they really angelic
flap their wings
dance at midnight
then you got down
to asking the real truth
you asked where they're from
their color and language
i think you should ask
the last person who smiled at you
offered a small favor
blessed your sneeze

CHAPTER THREE

It Happened Like This

The Satin Slip-Up by Lori Thatcher

When David and I decided to get married early in 1970, I said, "Let's keep it simple." Unlike many young women growing up in the sixties, I had never wasted time dreaming of the special day, fantasizing a fairy-tale gala. In fact, I disdained formality and harbored an arrogant, counter-culture contempt for the pretentiousness of pompous weddings. And then there was the reality of our finances. We were broke, and neither of our families could sponsor an extravagance.

David and I planned a small ceremony with a justice of the peace and then a weekend away at the ocean. Enter Margaret, my mother-in-law to be. Both of David's older sisters had eloped, and Margaret was craving a wedding where she could dress up and invite David's numerous relatives.

She wheedled: "Why not hold a small wedding and invite just a few relatives?"

She attempted to make us feel guilty: "I never got to be mother-of-the-bride; now you're taking away my chance to be mother-of-the-groom."

She threatened: "When you need my help, I'll remember you wouldn't do this one little thing for me."

David ducked, saying, "I don't care. The decision is yours and I'll support whatever you decide."

After some debate and fuss, I surrendered to the woman whom others in the family called "The General," and I began formulating a proper hippie wedding; it was after all, the Age of Aquarius.

We would marry on the first day of spring, check; the ceremony would be held outdoors, check; the site would be on top of a mountain, near the barn at Woolman Hill Quaker Conference Center, check. My bearded, long haired beau would wear a jacket, but no tie. The Unitarian minister would replace obey with cherish, and we would serve tea, veggie dishes, and whole wheat wedding cake.

When Margaret said she wanted to sew my wedding dress, I was intrigued. A hand-sewn garment could complete the artsy, earthy image I imagined.

I chose an off-white satin with a subtle, embossed paisley design and picked what I thought was a simple sewing pattern for a modest long dress. During the following months, I wasn't concerned that Margaret didn't have me try on the dress. I hadn't sewn anything, except for the apron and simple pullover shift I struggled through in home economics. I hadn't even been to a wedding, never mind participated in one. How would I know anything about the customary dress fittings? I assumed Margaret knew what she was doing.

When she had me try on the dress three days before the date, the garment was merely a white satin sack with arm holes and an uneven neckline. My mouth going dry, I stammered, "It still needs to be taken in and fitted. This doesn't look like the picture on the pattern."

Margaret muttered something about the impossibility of

darts. Finally, she stuck pins in it here and there and said, "I'm sure that'll take care of it."

There were no full length mirrors at her house, but the sack did feel a bit trimmer. Looking down and tugging a bit, I could make the neckline almost even.

Everything would be all right. How bad could it be, really?

Anyway, I had plenty else to fret about: Margaret wanted things her way, as usual, and we argued about everything. She insisted on preparing cold cut platters with bologna and ham and cheese, and she asked us to fork over money for food I didn't even want to serve. She tried to shame us, saying, "A lot of relatives are coming long distances and they expect to be well fed. Do you want them to say we starved them?" She expected us to have a ring bearer in the ceremony even though we hadn't planned one, and wanted us to ask the son of a distant relative we hadn't even met.

As if the wedding were as much hers as mine, she expected that for every suggestion I rejected, I should capitulate to another of her notions. I could hardly fret about the dress in midst of this struggle, and I sought to be too cool to fuss. Still, I felt apprehensive. Deep down, of course, I yearned to look pretty for my wedding.

I stopped to pick up the dress the night before the ceremony and Margaret handed me a wad of white satin balled up in a black trash bag, saying, "Finished! Now I can say I've sewn a wedding dress," as if she were crossing at item off her bucket list.

At the same time, she thrust a small package into my hand. At first I didn't recognize the white zipper with satin binding specified by the pattern—the one I had searched through store after store to locate.

I started to ask if she had used a different zipper, but Margaret was already hurrying away saying, "Lots to do. Lots to do."

She glanced back and added, as if an afterthought, "Well, I

wouldn't know how to put a zipper in, so you'll have to do that part."

My throat tightened. My mouth opened and closed like a landed salmon's. I barely squeaked out, "I don't know how to put zippers in."

She fished in her pocket and handed me a seam ripper. "Oh, you're smart, I'm sure you'll figure it out. But you'll probably need this."

I walked away stunned, even though I had yet to realize a mere zipper would do nothing to redeem the dress. After several hours, a murderous headache, and a bent seam ripper, the zipper was affixed and lay reasonably smoothly.

I tried on the dress.

Gazing at my reflection, I progressed from discouraged to depressed to despairing. Finally, I pulled the dress off and threw it onto the bed, my emotion leaping to pure fury—at both Margaret and toward her son as well.

David was nonplussed. He said, "Well," in a voice way too nonchalant for the situation. "Cancel the wedding, then. Or just wear something else." He was serious.

Cancel the wedding? That was crazy. What would we say? Margaret had invited every single relative she could contact. What would they think about us? David wasn't concerned, but I was.

Wear something else? I was a jeans and tee-shirt girl. I owned nothing else that even resembled a dress. Considering the argument that followed, it's amazing a wedding occurred.

When I ask myself now why I didn't agree to cancel or decide to wear something else, the only explanation I have is I was young and naïve—and timid. My family doctrine had taught me that it was useless for you to expect things to go your way in the world, so you might as well not cause a hullabaloo.

I was now beyond wanting to please my new mother-in-law, but not beyond my family principle of settling.

The next day, when my bridesmaid first saw me, she rushed over and hugged me for a long time. I was sure it was because she sought to hide the shock on her face.

I said, "I know. It's horrible," and she just hugged me tighter.

I was relieved snow had fallen the night before and the ceremony would be inside, in the foyer, where it was dark. There would be no aisle for me to walk down, and we would crowd together and face the minister with the guests scattered around in front of us.

I just wanted to get it over with.

At the reception, I shuddered whenever someone approached the head table, a small card table where just David and I sat. I felt a bit better when I noticed Margaret strutting around and heard her proclaim to one after another that she had made my dress. I hoped that explained it.

Thinking back, maybe my dress was perfect counterpoint to our best man's jeans and engineer boots and our four flower girls' unusual daisy headbands. Perhaps it harmonized with the rustic location with its board path spanning the stretch of mud in front of the door.

The dress didn't fit me, but it probably fit the start of our interesting, curious life together. Could it have been a good luck charm, even? Bad wedding dress heralds an enduring marriage? Forty-seven years later, I might smile about that lucky dress. Especially since it's only a memory now.

Our friend who photographed the wedding was using a darkroom in the barn at the conference center. He kept putting off printing the photos, but I was in no hurry to get them.

When the barn burned down months later, our wedding negatives were still hanging in the darkroom waiting to be printed. I heard it was an untended candle that started the fire. (I swear I didn't set it.)

Along with sadness at the loss of the beautiful structure, I felt utter relief. Fate had intervened, albeit at a great cost. I had already thrown the sad satin sack away, and now I would never have to hide my wedding pictures from friends or cringe over images of the worst-ever wedding dress.

A Right around Home Story by Estelle Cade

It was so hot that September day. School had just started after a long and extremely hot summer, and it was difficult to settle into the daily routine. "Stop acting so itchy" my mother said as I wandered around the house not even interested in my new reader from my new grade.

A strong wind had come up just as school let out. The sky had turned an odd shade of yellow and from our front porch we could see the flag pole in the schoolyard just across the street swaying back and forth, back and forth. "Will it break off, do you think?" my little sister whispered to me.

"Probably not, it's pretty strong" I assured her.

Dad arrived home from work a while later with a story of being buffeted by high winds as he drove across the Neponset Bridge and of the car "skittering" as he struggled against the winds as he drove along Wollaston Boulevard and to our street. "The tide is coming in", he said, "and the waves are beginning to crash against the sea wall."

Oh goody! Back we went to the front porch. By looking far down to the end of our street we could actually see the waves crashing up over the sea wall and onto the road! "Do you think there will be a flood? Will the ocean really come rushing down Beach Street?" My sister was full of questions with exciting possibilities.

The wind was blowing furiously by now - exhilarating to me, but mother opened the door, "You girls get in here right now and stay in. Do not go out on that porch again. It is dangerous."

After supper we retreated to our bedroom at the back of the house and busied ourselves with drawing and coloring, when suddenly there was a CRACK that stood our hair on end, followed by a THUD that sounded like the end of the world had come - then silence. (I have never forgotten the vibration of that sound, right through my feet.) Dad looked out the living room window and reported that the huge maple tree on the corner of the lot had been uprooted and had fallen just feet from our house!

The storm raged on all night; morning dawned sunny and clear. There was no school that day and neighbors and kids were out walking around, chatting and viewing the damage done – "watch out for live wires" was the word passed around. Considering that we lived on a tree-lined street, it was wonderful that homes had escaped the fury of the storm. Life soon returned to normal - and indeed, the flag pole stood sturdy and straight at our school yard.

And that was the Hurricane of September 9, 1938 as I recall it.

Dancing by Ted Scott

She looked like a movie star, all glamorous and made up, with lipstick, a short pretty dress, stockings and high heels. She looked 25 but was probably closer to 20, but to the two 15 year olds facing her she was smiling and friendly. She introduced herself as Betty. She would be our new dance teacher.

Donald and I had arrived at 10:00 on this Saturday morning. We had chained our bikes to a water pipe in back of the building and walked causally out to the front of the building, just across the street from the Hippodrome. We looked around carefully to make sure no one we knew could be in sight, then we quickly slipped inside the front door of the Arthur Murray Dance Studio.

Tired of being shy and not able to dance well, we had decided to learn how. Our parents had never even brought up the idea of dancing even though most of the other kids attended the occasional dances put on at the school.

I blame it on the preacher at our church. Although there was no Methodist doctrine saying "Thou shall not dance," he almost implied it by his severe and intolerant attitude on Sunday mornings. His favorite sermons were based on condemnation of the parishioners, how we were all going to Hell because of our unworthy souls.

Only God through Jesus Christ could save us and clearly most of us were too busy with worldly things to care. He was the most awful preacher we'd had yet, and we'd had some doozies.

I don't think that my parents considered dancing a sin. I'd actually caught them in the act once or twice after they got their Victrola. They always seemed kind of embarrassed about it. Maybe they thought it was just for married people.

I never even thought of bringing it up with them. They never had that sex talk with me and I'd had to learn it on my own from the Bible and Readers' Digest. So when Donald and I had discussed it, we decided to take the lessons on our own, after all we were both paperboys with good routes. We could afford it, and we didn't have to tell anyone about it.

It was a little surprising that there was only one other customer in the studio, a woman about 60 who was dancing with the guy who ran the place. He could have been our teacher's father. Donald and I would take turns dancing with the pretty lady.

Donald was up first. I watched, and noticed how easy it seemed. They were doing the waltz, and after a little confusion at the beginning it seemed like Donald just fell into it. But then I realized that Betty was trying to get Donald to lead. I realized that this was the hardest part of the lesson. Soon it was my turn, and Donald stepped away and Betty motioned for me to come forward. That was when I discovered that awful problem.

Betty had bad breath. I think back then they called it Halitosis, as if it were a disease. Of course like today they had a cure, but it wasn't on TV. No in that almost prehistoric time, they advertised on those signs you saw inside of buses. The slick cardboard signs that were about 2 feet wide and a foot long and rolled up into the bus's ceiling above the windows. There was no Google then, and almost no TV. Instead our supply of advertising content was nearly all from the insides of buses and from highway road signs.

As we danced, going through the same steps as she had with Don, the image in my mind changed, from dancing with a beautiful movie star to dancing with a witch from hell. No it wasn't that bad, but she had the worst case of Halitosis I'd ever seen. I almost had to keep my neck tilted back. We finished the lesson. We had paid for six lessons. We would be back at the same time next week.

When we got outside and checked that no one was watching, Donald said, "I thought I'd never get out of there. What did you think?"

"It was just as bad for me. I hope next time is better," I replied.

But the next week wasn't any better, so we never went back.

Years later, After reading an article about insects and their methods for eluding predators, I wondered if the Halitosis could have been a defensive mechanism, employed to keep strange service men from getting too close, while Betty waited for her boyfriend or fiancée to come home from the Korean War.

I have Arrived by Lettice Randall

It was the fall of 1961. I had recently begun my sophomore year at Newmarket High school. My family had moved to Newmarket, New Hampshire a couple of years earlier, and although I had many new friends and felt reasonably secure in my new school, I was still a little shy and very nervous about doing anything that would call attention. This is why I surprised even myself when I decided to try out for a play that my English teacher was going to be directing. This would be Mr. K's first attempt at putting on a play, so there were going to be a lot of firsts for both of us.

The day of tryouts came. I auditioned for a couple of parts and was excited to be chosen for the part of Alice, mother of one of the leading characters. The play was called *Death Takes a Holiday*. I only vaguely remember the plot. It seems "Death" in human form desires to see what love is all about. He decides to visit earth as a human for three days to see what he can learn. He ends up falling in love with the daughter of the people who have opened their home to him. His identity is found out and he is asked to leave. He will, but only if the daughter goes with him. She does, meaning she dies. This is where I find my moment of fame as the girl's mother. I'm supposed to cry over my daughter's demise. As I got into my role and studied my lines, I spent a fair amount of time trying to figure out how I would convince the audience that I was really crying. How could I make it sound convincing? Then I had an idea. Earlier that summer, my eight year old cousin Jimmy had been killed when he darted into the road in front of an oil truck in Shelburne Falls. I had a very difficult time dealing with this when it happened and just thinking about it would bring me to tears. That was how I'd make myself cry. I'd think of Jimmy.

The night of the play came. The play was going ok, but perhaps dragging a little. Mr. K was a bit disappointed in the performance and tried to motivate us as best he could, hoping it might pick things up a little. Finally it was near the end of the play and time for my crying scene which was the last scene of the play. I started my lines, paused, and thought of my young cousin and how much I missed him. It worked. The tears truly started flowing. I just had to be sure I didn't get so carried away that no one could understand what I was saying. I managed to get through my rather lengthy set of lines with just the right amount of weepiness. It was perfect. As the play ended and the cast members all came out, one by one, to take a bow, Mr. K clapped especially hard for me as did the audience. I was elated beyond measure. Mr. K was beaming. His first attempt at directing a play ended up being a huge hit. As a side benefit to this, I tried out for and acted in many more plays. Gone was the shy girl who was always cautious about bringing attention to herself. I became bold and more sure of myself. At the end of that school year I gave Mr. K my yearbook to sign. Imagine how my confidence grew when I read what he had written. "Lettice, I will always remember you and your wonderful performance in *Death Takes a Holiday*. You gave me une raison d'etre. (A reason to be.)

I had arrived!

Maiden Voyage of the SS Glaser by Marty Glaser

In 1971, I bought a 1965 Trade Winds tent trailer which slept six. I asked my dad if he would like to go with me on the maiden voyage of the SS Glaser. Being a good sport as well as good company, he agreed. We drove to the back of Otis Air Force base, got to the campground, and set up our home on wheels. God must have had a sense of humor. Just when we had finished, it started pouring. We were unaware that a hurricane was blowing through Otis. We were dry, but disappointed.

The trees bent at a sixty degree angle, blown by winds raging like a sea storm. Mud began accumulating under the metal stair while the tent trailer bobbed and weaved like a tiny flower.

Around midnight, I got up to go to the bathroom, which was a quarter mile walk from our campsite. I stepped off the metal stairs and oozed into mud up to my knees. I was shocked and soaked but not discouraged yet. I returned, walking like an old man with a load in his pants. I finally reached the trailer, strode up the stairs, opened the door and walked in. My dad just stared at me.

Rain continued falling for the next two days. The first morning, my dad had to go to the bathroom. He stepped off the metal stairs, as I did, and sunk into the muddy ooze up to his knees, just like I had. He was wet, cold, and in shock. Watching my father knee deep in the mud, I could see that he was not happy and thought perhaps we had camped for both the first and the last time.

Dad walked to the bathroom. He returned from the bathroom. Even through the pounding rain, I understood every word he was yelling. I don't know if he addressed anyone in particular or just spoke to God, complaining about me.

I heard him say quite clearly, "Some children take their parents to Florida. My son takes me to a hurricane!"

At that moment, I realized that whatever fun I had hoped to have with my dad was dashed. I would have to be content to travel with friends if I ever expected to use the trailer again. Dad would never, ever, go with me on another camping trip.

Leaving Home by Janet Keyes

It was to be our lifetime home. We started in 1960 fixing up all four rooms (and one bathroom and no closets) with scrubbing cleansers, elbow grease, paint and wallpaper. It was a perfect place for newlyweds. In 1968 we accommodated our growing family by adding two bedrooms, a dining room, and another bathroom, plus six closets. Our lives exhilarated in optimism and pride.

Gradually the house deteriorated some. The door into the living room could not stay closed, for 27 years. The finish on the dining room and kitchen floors became worn and shabby. The living room carpet smelled vaguely musty. I became discouraged and finally one Christmas I told my husband I wanted only one thing—a braided rug for the living room as a promise that we would refurbish these three rooms during the following year.

Two-thousand-six was a fabulous year. New cherry floors glowed throughout the downstairs. We even broke out a wall and created an airy sun room addition to the dining room. We spent too much, but we were on top of the world. Our house was exactly as we wanted it, and we knew we could finish out our lives in our beloved home with all its memories.

Then life happened. For a lot of good reasons we had to build a new house on the other side of town. The frustrations of that process are spelled out in a twelve-chapter book I have half written. Over several months we sorted, cleaned, re-organized, discarded, donated, evaluated, eliminated, boxed, labeled, and bagged. When moving day finally came the day after we got our certificate of occupancy, we were too tired to experience much emotion. I had designed the new house to incorporate all of our favorite features of the old house, so leaving the old home behind and embracing life in our new home was blessedly easy. Our memories and our ghosts came with us. It was truly a homecoming, and we never again referred to the old house as "home."

Bee Incentive by Mildred Grant

Memory tells me there were no barways in the stone walls between the three pastures on the north side of the driveway at Great Uncle Merritt's lovely 1700's colonial home in Heath where my mother took us to spend our summer vacation. Since the memory of a seven or eight year old could be faulty, I realize there must have been gates of some kind to allow passage from one hay field to the next by a herd of cattle or haying equipment. There were horses to pasture, too.

From the kitchen window, Mom had a clear view of the cattle barn, across the three pastures, and up to the town road. As the first batch of doughnuts went into the deep kettle of hot fat on the old wood-fired iron stove, Mom noticed her four older children, Chester, Eleanor, Mildred, and Allen were climbing over the second stone wall, headed for the last barrier to the town road.

"Clara, are you busy?" Mom asked.

A pretty young girl in her pre-teens appeared in the kitchen doorway, a slender finger marking her place in the book she was carrying.

"No, Aunt Helen, I'm just scanning a book. I hope there is something I can do for you," said Clara.

"Would you please go up the driveway and remind the children that this side of that last stone wall is the limit of their territory for exploration in that direction?" Mom asked.

"That I'm sure I can do, as long as I can leave the doughnut frying in the hands of an expert."

Clara went out the back door to follow in the footsteps of her cousins, trying to place her feet where they would do the least damage to the ripening hay. Glancing ahead, she noticed Chet, last over the third stone wall, lingering and peering back at the base of the wall.

As Clara caught up with the children, she said, "Your Mother asked me to remind you that this is as far as you are allowed to go in this direction. What were you looking at below the wall here, Chet?" she asked.

"Oh, nothing. I thought I saw a small snake," Chet lied, passing his interest off as he turned to his brother and sisters, asking, "What will we do now that we can't cross the road?"

"What were you going to do across the road that you can't do right here?" Clara asked.

Eleanor spoke up, saying, "We're collecting old dry pine and hemlock cones for Mom to start the fire in the morning, but there aren't any more on this side of the road."

Clara suggested, "Let's bring string with us tomorrow morning and bundle all these downed, dry small branches that will make good fire starters. Now, I need to know whether any of you know how to make an Indian scalp."

Not to be left out, Allen asked, "Find an Indian and cut off the top of his head?"

None of the rest of us could come up with a better idea.

Clara said, as she walked up close to the lower branches of a hemlock tree, "Here's how you do it. This will work only if the new, bright green growth is on the ends of the branches, like this. Grasp the end of the branch with your left hand, with your right hand peel off a small circle of the bark about four inches up from the end of the branch. Now, with the branch still in your left hand and your right thumbnail pressed on the part where you peeled the bark off, pull toward you. See?" Clara shook out the limp "scalp" and pointed to the skeleton twigs where the "scalp" had been.

After several tries we each managed to make our very own "scalp". The poor tree might never recover, but Mom calling us to lunch saved it further defoliation. Chester poked Allen and dared him to a race back to the house.

Starting forward, Chet egged Allen on, saying, "You have to jump over the stone walls, too," as he more than cleared the first hurdle.

Spurred on by his big brother's taunts, Allen mustered all his physical resources into a ball of furious energy and went full tilt toward the stone wall. He almost cleared the barrier, but lost his momentum near the end of the jump. His back took some scrapes and bruises as he slid down the rock wall to land with a resounding thump. Trying not to cry over the painful scrapes, he suddenly heard loud buzzing sounds and felt sharper, stinging pains from the ground dwelling bees that were objecting to the sudden intrusion to their peaceful home. Screaming, arms flailing, Allen surged to his feet and headed to the house at such a pace that he cleared the remaining stone walls with ease, leaving his big brother to "eat his dust".

Doughnuts fried, a large batch of "Cry Baby" molasses cookies, spread out to cool, plus a meat and vegetable casserole almost ready for lunch, Mom felt the morning had been well spent. Just as she was congratulating herself on the sights and smells around her, Allen's terrified screams took over every other sound and thought. Rushing to the back door, she saw him fly over the stone wall beyond the driveway. Now thoroughly alarmed and puzzled, she wondered what could possibly be the reason for his actions.

"Mama, Mama, bees," Allen sobbed as he clung to his mother.

First comforting him, and then checking for hitchhiking bees, Mom remembered the mud puddle left after yesterday's shower. From her kneeling position, she reached the still wet earth and began plastering every bee sting she could see.

Panting, the remaining children came to a standstill, Chester hanging back from the rest.

Looking up, Mom asked, "Clara and Eleanor, please wring out clean dish towels with water from the barrel in the kitchen. His eyes are swelling shut. The cold water should help keep the swelling down."

Cousin Clara, who was watching Chester, and wondering whether to mention his previous knowledge of the bee's nest, decided to tell her Aunt Helen when she saw Chet turn away from the group, headed for the barn with a smug mocking smile on his face. Uncle Furb would be coming up from Greenfield tomorrow, for the weekend. Maybe then he and Aunt Helen would do something about the situation.

Mrs. McOwen by Noreen O'Brien

Mrs. McOwen was extremely tall, exceedingly thin. Her hair, pulled straight and taut against her scalp and rolled into a tight flip from one earlobe round the back to the other, looked like a gray, hairy tootsie roll. Her half glasses sat on a sharply pointed beak of a nose and her face, squinched up at all times in a grimace, was home to a wart on one cheek. Her bony hands smelled like commercial strength girls' room soap, that yellow-green goop.

Although I hated her long, straight skirts, silky blouses, cardigan sweaters and eyeglass chain, I loved her shoes. Black with thick, wide high heels, her shoes made lovely solid clunks as she walked across the wooden third-grade classroom floor. Perhaps I was looking for something to love about Mrs. McOwen and loving her shoes was safe.

I had my first out-of-body experience in Mrs. McOwen's class—at least, the first of which I have a clear recollection. An ugly boil on the back of my right leg was large and most painful; indeed, I still have the scar. My parents did not take me to a doctor; rather, Uncle Shawn drenched the area in rubbing alcohol and poked the boil with a sewing needle to lance it. I was terrified, and though I wouldn't expose my terror to them by screaming—my terror rained down my cheeks in silent tears.

However, Uncle Shawn, just a few years older than I, laughed at me, calling me a baby. My parents joined him in the teasing, though in all likelihood, they meant only to lance the bubble of the stress of the moment with laughter. As my uncle approached me with that needle, I know I left my body, though the memory of it is not as vivid as that of the next day in Mrs. McOwen's classroom.

Mrs. McOwen loved to humiliate me in front of the class. She was merciless. Struggling to see the numbers of the long division problems on the blackboard, I felt panic over having just broken my pencil as I scribbled on my math paper; this, after having rubbed a hole in it with my much-used nub of an eraser, evidence that I was struggling.

Limping across the classroom toward the front corner of the room, I was lost in a knot of anxiety, wishing for a clean piece of paper to begin again to hide the proof of my struggle from Mrs. McOwen. I was barely aware that I had passed another student who was coming from the sharpener nailed to the sill of the window closest to Mrs. McOwen's desk.

Mrs. McOwen pointed at me as I returned to my seat saying in a mocking tone, "Monkey see, monkey do." Having no idea what she meant, but knowing I was the butt of her nastiness, I felt tiny, ugly and stupid, wishing I was invisible—and not a monkey.

The sound of my classmates laughing rang in my ears, but seemed to move far off, gaining distance as I got closer to my seat at the rear of the class. For the first time, I was thankful that Mrs. McOwen had moved me to almost the last seat in the class where no one could see me once I was past them, though it was agonizing passing at the speed of a slug those long rows of laughing faces.

Without warning, I found some part of myself suspended just below the ceiling, but under the hanging lights, looking down where I sat in my seat, diminutive, head down, pained face covered by fine, straight hair, tiny shoulders hunched in an attempt to curl into a fetal position at my desk. My fingers, from nervous manipulation of my pencil, were gray and dirty with powdery lead. I wore a plaid skirt and white blouse, my right leg stuck out in the aisle at an awkward angle, oozing pus peeping through the gauze taped around my calf. My heart broke for the ugly, skinny, stupid little girl, isolated and alone.

Cutting myself off from my parents, Mrs. McOwen, other children, I was safe. Stunned—relieved—to discover that they did not, could not, see me, I realized that what they did see was only a shell of me, a container, an ugly little worthless coating, that answered to my name. They could hurt the outer shell, stabbing me with needles, hitting me with the belt, humiliating me, however, the inner me, the real me, was safe, high above them.

It was exhilarating to know that I had the power to create a safety zone. I had a place to turn for cover; I did not have to count on anyone for protection. No longer would I turn for help and find a vacuum.

i didn't know by Alice Thomas

while i was preparing for the day
brushing and such   i heard soft voices
like those that croon the morning light
watch for filters of dust and work-reminders
they leap into the kitchen to smooth the stove
move the spoon   just before the sun
they gloss my hair then wrap the light
across your face - i didn't know you were so handsome

A Rite of Passage by Dolly Arsenault

At first, my new husband and I always visited our respective families together. Then, a few months after our wedding in 1966, I had a day off from work but Al didn't. I was lonely and had an unexpected yearning to see my family. So, I scribbled my husband a note telling him where I'd be and asking him to come by when he got out of work.

I didn't bother to phone before I took off for the home I'd known for twenty-two years. My two youngest sisters should be there. Their school year had ended and, at 13 and 15 they were too young to have summer jobs. Most likely they'd be watching TV. I looked forward to spending some girl time with them, and staying long enough to see my father, brother and other sisters when they arrived from work.

I didn't drive then, but I lived a mere mile away and sprinted most of it. Being young, fit, and impatient, I made it in record time.

Our house didn't have a window in the back door, so we'd

made it a practice to always use the front door which did have a window and which allowed us to peek before answering. Both doors were only locked at night or if no one was home. (It was a safer era and neighborhood then.) So, on this, my first solo visit, I stomped up the front steps. I knew someone would hear and check out that I was friend not foe. I spent a few moments on the porch huffing and puffing until I got my wind back.

The adjacent living room window was open and I heard music coming from the television. I smiled. Oh yes, Mary and Imelda were home.

My hand automatically reached for the doorknob—but hovered there while I tried to determine if I should turn it. What was the protocol? Was I supposed to knock first? If I were a guest, well, of course. But I was still a family member, wasn't I? When Al and I had visited together, this hadn't been a consideration. On those occasions, we'd been expected, and my beaming father had greeted us with both the door and his arms wide open.

Before I could decide what to do, my sister Mary opened the door.

"Hey," she said, frowning. "I saw you coming up the stairs. Why didn't you just come on in?"

I flushed. "You know...I wasn't sure I could just come in. I thought maybe I should knock or ring the bell."

Mary waved me toward the living room. "'Course not! Dolly, c'mon in. Imelda and I are watching 'The Million Dollar Movie.' Today they're showing something with Judy Garland and there's lots of singing and dancing and stuff. You'll love it."

I sat in an armchair and along with my sisters, soon became immersed in the musical. Mary waited for a commercial before she elbowed her younger sister sitting beside her.

"Guess what, Mel," she said with a grin. "Dolly thought she had to ring the bell when she came."

They both had a belly laugh. Then Imelda turned to me

and asked, "Geez, this is your home. Why would you think that?"

I shrugged and didn't bother to answer. Had I thought, I would have told them: just wait until it's your turn to leave the family. See if you feel comfortable just popping in. This won't be your home once you go. It simply won't.

Running Late by Marty Glaser

While working at The Stetson Home for Boys School in Barre, Ma, I also took graduate studies at Fitchburg State College. One day I was running late and thought I would take a short cut and shave twenty minutes off the travel time. Then I could get to Fitchburg in plenty of time for my class.

I drove over a hill and saw glare ice all the way to the bottom. My 1971 Pinto hatchback slipped to the right towards a rut in the road and started picking up speed. It seemed inevitable that I was going to crash.

As my car slid towards the telephone pole at the bottom of the icy road, I silently prayed I could yank the Pinto free. I frantically downshifted from third, to second, to first but my speed continued to increase. I yanked up the hand brake so hard that it came off in my hand. I had absolutely no control over my car.

I hurtled towards disaster and possibly my death and my life flashed before my eyes. Still, the thought came to mind that if I lived, I would have to pay for damage to the pole—$250.00.

I tightened my seat belt, crossed my hands on the steering wheel, and put my head down to protect my head and face. As I tore the telephone pole off its base, I had to be going forty miles an hour. When the car finally stopped, the pole had dented a perfect arch where the hood had been.

The odd thing was that I was still alive.

Then I realized I would be late for graduate school classes and knew I'd be big trouble with my special education professors.

First, I had to get to a phone and call a tow truck to take the car to Stanley's Auto Body Shop in Athol.

I spotted a trailer and trudged through the snow. I knocked and an elderly woman met me at the door.

"Mam, I just had an accident. May I please use your phone to call for a tow truck?"

She looked me straight in the face and said the words which still linger in my memory as if it were yesterday: "You could have used my phone, but YOU BROKE THE POLE AND THE TELEPHONE LINES ATTACHED TO THE POLE!"

I mumbled apologies for having caused her distress, turned and walked down the road about five miles to the next house. The people there were kind and let me call the tow truck.

Because I was in such a hurry to get to graduate school, I did not pass go, didn't collect $200, and took several steps backwards instead.

In Hiding by Lori Thatcher

Sun shining through gaps between boards in the barn wall sparkled a storm of hay dust as I stirred the air by moving my hand back and forth. The day was warm and my bed of hay bales soft. It was my favorite place to spend time after doing the barn chores.

I might have been daydreaming, although if you had asked me then, I probably would have said I was just looking at stuff: the spot-lit dust, the yellow-green hay whose color predicted how it smelled, and the scenes I could see through the gaps in the barn wall—like little slices of the world.

I didn't have a book with me like I usually did, but I might have been thinking about the perfect word to describe something I was looking at. I had recently realized that knowing the right word was half like a defense and half like magic. I'm pretty sure I wasn't thinking about school. Junior high was proving tougher than I had hoped and most of the time I found it easier to ignore.

When I heard my father's voice call, "Lori," as he walked down the path from the house I shared with my mother and siblings, I flinched. I wasn't supposed to climb on top of the hay.

My father had lectured my younger brother and me, saying climbing on the hay loosened the bail strings, but I saw no harm in it. I was the one who pulled down the bales and shook out the tightly packed sections of hay during morning and night feedings for our two horses.

I had plenty of time to scramble from my perch without getting caught there, but hearing my name called a second time, closer, I froze, and decided to hide from my father.

I thought my father would look for me for a few minutes and then go back to his car and return to the house a few miles down the road where he had lived with his sister and her family ever since he and my mother separated. But I heard rustling and hammering and realized he was doing something barely ten feet away in the center aisle of the small barn. He might have even been able to see my knees if he had craned his neck and looked up on top of the pile of hay bales.

Once in a while he would go to the barn door, look outside and call my name.

Dust filled my lungs. My chest rattled as I wheezed into my sleeve willing myself not to sneeze or cough. My leg cramped and I stretched it out slowly, cringing at the crackle the hay made. Sweat ran into my eyes and suddenly I had to pee.

At one point, my father said, "That half-assed bitch." I assumed he was talking about my mother; I had heard him call her half-assed before. But I had never heard him use the word *bitch*. Did he mean me? This overhearing seemed to make my deception grow from mild disobedience to inexcusable transgression.

My father probably stayed only an hour but time seemed never-ending, every minute stretched by my growing discomfort. Finally I heard him talking to the horses outside the barn door and then there was silence. I stretched my sore legs out but waited a long time to creep down to see whether he was actually gone.

I remember shaking my head, baffled at why I hid in the first place, baffled at why it made me feel so terribly small.

It wasn't clear to me then that hiding can diminish a person. I only knew that after feeling imprisoned there, my secret place no longer felt special or safe, and I never again climbed up on the hay.

Like the slices of the world I saw through the cracks between barn boards, my understanding was a chopped up picture. Still, even at that time, I thought it puzzling that giving up hiding felt less like a loss and more like a trade-off.

When I went back up to the house, my mother said, "Lori. Your father was looking for you."

I said, "I know." I was glad she didn't ask me to explain.

A Minor Triumph by David Allen Bryant

About two months after my uncle's death, I decided to go back to New Jersey to see how my aunt was doing, since she was now alone in a fairly big house. It was early spring, and I decided to travel by bus.

I didn't bring any money with me. There was money in my bank account here, and I thought I could just go to a bank in New Jersey as soon as I got there. To my utter surprise, the banks closed at one-o'clock on Saturdays in New Jersey. But I was sure I could get by until Monday. After all, my aunt had always provided anything a family member needed.

When I got to my aunt's house, I could see she was very upset. I learned that my uncle had left some loose ends after a previous marriage, and this was bothering her. As we sat talking about it, I became very tired—too tired to continue talking, and I told her that. All of a sudden she seemed to snap, and she jumped to her feet shouting in a rage, "Get out! Get out!"

I headed out the door with no money and nowhere to go. I had not had any contact with other relatives in New Jersey, so I found myself stranded at least until the following Monday.

I walked the streets until dusk. By nightfall I had grown very tired. I decided to go back to my aunt's house, thinking maybe she felt better. I knocked and knocked, but there was no answer and the house was dark. I decided to sleep on the front porch.

One thing I have relied on is my faith in God to see me through hard times. It was a long, cold night after all, and I had no blanket and just a light jacket. I tossed and turned all night, but the Lord got me through it.

I was awakened to the sound of birds chirping, and the radiant sun smiling down on me. Across the street there was an apartment where friends of my aunt lived. I went there and told them my story. They cheerfully agreed to let me stay with them until I could get some money. They gave me food, shelter, and a place to shower. They were so kind I decided to stay a couple days longer.

Finally I got to a bank and got money, and I departed. Since then I have never traveled without spare cash. I thank my heavenly Father for this minor triumph.

Black Bird Eating Seeds of Sumac by Sherry Payne Kohler

Bird black curve on a branch
Seed red curve toward the sky

Snow white fall on the earth
Pure gold day of a life

Bird black day of my life
Seed red sumac to share

Snow white light under sun
Bare feet feather to fly.

CHAPTER FOUR

Sounds, Light, Action

Kelly Green by Janice Lepore

Whatever possessed me to buy bright Kelly green sneakers? It was many years ago, during my monotone phase, and some would say it must have been the price—on sale, that is—or perhaps something to do with St. Patrick's Day. But what in the world did I think I would wear them with?

I'm well known for "Sally Boutique" bargains that kept me and my expanding brood clothed through the years. My daughters roll their eyes at some of my unique restyling projects, but maintain that I look fine when I lay aside my sometimes unusual home clothes and join the outside world.

My contention that if I alter all the unflatteringly snug clothes (you know, "tight") to a comfort level, then I will eventually lose weight has yet to be confirmed.

I digress. The issue here is the like-new pair of green sneakers fondly known as G'ma's clown shoes. Why they fit my list of keepsakes, I'll never know. I have collections of dolls, pens, letter openers, picture frames, clocks, paperweights, music boxes, Santa Clauses, and more bells than I can ever count—none of which I am ready to part with in the annual neighborhood tag sale.

There's also that pewter locket with the blue stone that I purchased with my first real paycheck at eighteen, much to my parent's dismay. I consider it an heirloom. After all, that was over fifty years ago.

Those green sneakers still command a place of honor in the one and only hanging shoe bag. They haven't been paraded at Halloween in recent years, as ballerina and witch costumes have been in vogue. My kids grew up in the 60s and 70s when fun was using your imagination to dress in hobo or clown attire. There was always competition to see who got to wear the ugly shoes.

Now that I finally think that wearing those bright green shoes might be appropriate with a colorful outfit, I have another problem. How do I shrink my feet to a 7 1/2?

A Summer's Eve by Cathey Boschen

Dusk, descending over the yard,

The evening heavy with the heat of the day.

A young girl sits on a swing, gently swaying,

Her little brother is on the swing set glider, slowly pumping back and forth,

Trying to create a breeze.

They wait quietly for the darkness of night,

A cricket begins to chirp, a mosquito buzzes by,

Trees and bushes become shadows and shapes, and then disappear.

As the darkness of night surrounds them, little lights begin to appear,

> Blinking on and off, moving from space to space.

And the children, once hot and tired, jump up with renewed energy.

The yard is filled with the magic of fire flies.

Elusive, evasive.

With laughter and anticipation the children run and reach out to catch them,

> Never quite close enough,

> Yet boasting about the one that got away.

Occasionally there is a gift of one close by that they capture in the cup of their hands

Then they peer within in wonder,

at the little twinkling light with its luminous glow.

Satisfied, they release it and continue on with renewed enthusiasm and determination,

> Chasing the elusive, magic lights in the night.

Aromas From my Childhood by Marty Glaser

To this day, I can recall the aromas wafting out of my Bubbe Jenny's kitchen. She was always cooking, and everything she cooked, baked, broiled, or slow cooked in Rokeach tomato sauce smelled and tasted divine.

Thursday afternoons were hectic days for Bubbe and Aunt

Bertha. They were responsible for cooking all of the food to be served on Friday night. I would help Bubbe prepare the chicken, brisket, potatoes, vegetables, and Challah. Bubbe Jenny taught me to knead the dough, twist it into a pattern and then bake it in the oven. Smelling all the food drove my nose crazy and set my mouth salivating.

Another job was to help Aunt Bertha set the table for six: my mother, my father, Jerry, me, Bubbe Jenny, and Aunt Bertha.

Usually we would have the courses in order: gefilte fish, chopped liver, chicken soup with matzoh balls, baked chicken, tsimmes, slow roasted brisket, and assorted vegetables. Once the main meal dishes were cleared, dessert and coffee or tea was served.

On Friday night before the evening meal, we took showers and dressed up to welcome Sabbath as the Crowning creation of God. When all was ready in the kitchen, and everyone was seated, my mother lit the two Sabbath candles, and while covering her face with her hands, recited the Hebrew prayer. Then my father said the blessings over the wine and the Challah. After the prayer, father cut the Challah and passed it down the line until everyone had a piece.

After the meal, Jerry and I helped Bubbe and Aunt Bertha bring the dirty dishes into the kitchen. Once we had done our last chore, we got ready to go to Temple with our father for the Friday night service at eight o'clock.

Jerry and I made sure our hair was combed, and we had clean pants and a clean shirt with a tie that matched. The last thing was to shine our shoes.

We were told that when we went to Temple Israel, we represented our parents, Aunt Bertha and Bubbe Jenny, and that our behavior reflected how our parents brought us up. We were not allowed to wear dungarees on Friday eve or Saturday morning when the Torah was taken out of the Ark and read. We were instructed to be on our best behavior because father was a dentist and a well-respected member of the Christian and Jewish communities.

Father drove us to Temple. We walked up the steps to the side door and Father kissed the Mezuzah on the door lintel. Jerry and I did the same. I still kiss the Mezuzah when I enter and leave our house. It reminds us Jews of the bitterness of slavery and the sweetness of freedom.

I usually couldn't stay awake and would fall asleep on the old wooden pews, a prayer book for my pillow. Father was frustrated that I was not participating in the service, but Rabbi Ucko calmed my father's concerns, saying, "If Marty feels comfortable falling asleep on a wooden bench with a prayer book for his pillow, don't worry about him growing up to know he is Jewish. He will want to be Jewish and will surprise you all!"

After the service, I woke up to sweet aromas floating down the stairs. The ladies of the Temple were serving delicious cookies, and pies. I walked upstairs and my eyes almost popped out of my head. The desserts looked and smelled wonderful, but we had to wait until our elders served themselves. I waited patiently, even though I would have liked to grab the food and run off. But I didn't want to listen to another lecture about good behavior.

To this day I am a very observant and religious Jew. I feel very comfortable being Jewish and entering any temple.

The Baton Rouge Jail, late March in 1957 by Ted Scott

The highpoint of my stay was the second night in jail, when I dreamed about food. I dreamed of a meal at Aunt Elsie's small farm in Athens in East Tennessee. I'd almost forgotten, but the dream was so real that I knew I'd never forget.

I was 10 or 11, and we were all there, my cousins, our parents, my sister and me, and our beloved hostess, my Great Aunt Elsie.

There were all of my favorites, green beans cooked with a little pork and that special seasoning that I never tasted anywhere else, except once at a small restaurant in Roxbury that drew me in with its smell.

There were big thick red slices of tomatoes fresh off the vine. There was also fried okra, and smooth sweet mashed potatoes dripping with butter and swimming in gravy.

There was sweet yellow corn just picked and cooked on the cob, and delicious big pieces of southern fried chicken, and a cold tall glass of sweetened ice tea.

And those fluffy hot homemade biscuits and rolls.

At the end there were piles of thinly sliced watermelon with seeds, and the wonderful buttery chocolate pie that all of us craved.

The smells were so good that only the taste could be better.

I hated to wake up from the dream.

I already knew what my breakfast would be. A cup of chicory, a small bowl of unsweetened grits and maybe a piece of dirty white bread. But I knew it would be the best meal of the day, and I was hungry and ready to eat.

Get a Move On by Lettice Randall

It was early September of 1964. My parents and I lived in Newmarket NH, and I had graduated from high school there the previous June. My dad had recently begun working at the Great

Bay Training Center in Portsmouth where he had a wood working class for boys with developmental delays. Because of this, we would soon be moving to Portsmouth.

I was not happy about this prospect. All my friends were in Newmarket, and because I was in the middle of a nasty case of mononucleosis, it would be a while before I could borrow Mom's car and drive to visit anyone. The other thing that bothered me was that my steady boyfriend, Charlie, who was in the Navy, had just set sail for a three month Mediterranean cruise so I wouldn't be seeing him for a while either.

We finally moved into our new place on Greenland Road in Portsmouth. It wasn't bad as apartments go. It was in a large duplex with big rooms both upstairs and down. The neighborhood was quiet and on the outskirts of the city, and the house set well back from the street protected from the usual traffic noises. The only drawback was that it was right near the Pease Air Force Base, so there would be some noise from airplanes coming and going. For whatever reason, this didn't prove to be a bothersome issue, although one day a plane crashed on takeoff and landed right on the highway near our home.

I survived the long fall, and by January I was well enough to go back to my job at Sylvania Electric in Exeter. I would ride with a lady from Portsmouth who also worked there. At least I'd have a little more human contact. Also, now I was going to be able to get to Newmarket to see my friends. And my boyfriend had recently returned from the Med cruise. I thought that I might survive after all.

Ok, now move ahead three months. It's April. I'm home with my parents one evening when the phone rings. It's Charlie calling from Boston where he's stationed on the USS Wasp. Seems he wants to break up. Seems he thinks we should see other people. Jerk! I hang up on him and send the phone on a flying trip. It didn't go too far. Remember, phones had cords in those days.

The next day is Saturday. I'm so miserable. First, I'm living with my parents in Portsmouth. Second, my idiot boyfriend has just dumped me!

"Mom, can I borrow your car? I'd like to go to Newmarket and visit Patsy and Bruce." Patsy and Bruce had graduated from high school with me and were good friends of both me and Charlie. They had married right out of high school and had an apartment in a large building owned by a Mr. Mungeon. It was affectionately known as Mungeon's Dungeons.

I called Patsy and Bruce and, yes, they were going to be home. "Come on over. We'd love to see you. You can spend the day with us."

So I was on my way. Newmarket or bust. I made the 15 mile drive in record time, hoping Mom wouldn't find out which would put an end to my borrowing her car, forever.

I got to Patsy and Bruce's and filled them in about my recent breakup with Charlie and how much I detested Portsmouth and how boring it was living with my parents, even though, as parents went, they were pretty good. But, I added that I needed my independence, after all I was 18. I wasn't getting any younger!

"Hey," Patsy interjected, "There's an empty apartment upstairs right over us. It's a studio but it's a big one. It just recently went up for rent. We could go down to Mr. Mungeon's apartment and see if he'll show it to you. What do you think?"

"Wow! That would be great. Yes, let's do it." So down to Mr. Mungeon's we went, and yes, he'd show it to me. If I wanted it, it would be available in three weeks.

I looked at the apartment. It was furnished, even including a TV. The rent was $12.50 a week which included heat. I could afford this on my $46 a week salary (after taxes). I took it.

The deal was done. I was moving back to Newmarket. Suddenly all the bad things of the last few months took a back seat. Now I had something to look forward to. Now I could become an independent adult. Now I had to tell my parents. Gulp!

I returned to Portsmouth that evening, nervous about telling my parents. Would they give me a hard time? Would they disapprove? Of course, even if they did, there wasn't much they could do about it. After all, I was an 18 year old adult. And I was ready to pay my own way in the world.

Well, imagine my surprise when Mom said, "Good for you. I tell you what, on Monday night I'll bring you shopping for some things you're going to need in your new apartment. And my dad? He gave me $10 to use toward buying some of the items I'd need.

Was it my imagination, or did my parents seem just a little too excited about my move? Hmmm.

About three months after my move, Charlie wrote me a letter apologizing for being such an idiot and saying he wanted to get back together. I didn't have to think twice. Yes, yes, a thousand times yes! Three months later we were married. October 17, 1965.

Lights of my Life by Janet Keyes

In my earliest memory of light I was a toddler wrapped in my mother's arms as I peered over her shoulder at pale daylight beyond the kitchen windows.

Next, I recall fireflies, lightning bugs twinkling at twilight, first in the grass, then in a glass jar on a summer evening until we released them to commune with each other and compete with the stars.

As a young child I delighted in the autumn hay dust brightly dancing in narrow shafts of sunlight squeezing through cracks between barn boards.

In later childhood I marveled at lightning flashing

benevolently over August's eastern horizon through long summer evenings, silent, and too distant to be scary.

As a teen, I celebrated dappled sunlight dimpling between lawn shadows of leaves stirred by slight breezes.

Later on, I wondered at the wings of the morning, shafts of sunlit moisture drawn upward from dewy grass to fluffy clouds in the sky.

As a young adult I smiled at the flash of Allan's camera as he took my picture, then I took his, that evening when he first told me he loved me.

Before long, I was napping with my first baby, and she watched as my eyes opened, and her face lit up with her first spontaneous smile of joy.

A few years later our family breathlessly watched the northern lights, the aurora borealis, swirling and undulating green, red, yellow, and violet back and forth across the summer night sky.

During many winters, we shared sunlit sparkles of millions of frozen diamonds scattered across fields of new snow, and gleaming icy baubles glowing on every branch and twig.

Sometimes we mulled over the mysteries of lights lurking and darting in pasture and woods where no light source existed.

After the darkest night of our lives, we welcomed the dawn light bringing comfort and hope after a long and sleepless night of grief and tears.

On cold nights we cherish the flickering flames behind the glass door of our wood stove, gently warming the whole house. Now we treasure memories of the glorious and ever-changing lights of a thousand sunrises and sunsets over the years.

The Sea Never Leaves Us by Estelle Cade

We reach the crest of the Big Green Bridge,
crossing from New Hampshire into Maine.
Three pairs of small hands reach out from the back -
Who'll be the first one into Maine?
Always Dad, of course -
He's driving!

"I see the ocean!"
a voice from the back seat.
Heads swivel - yes!
The first glimpse of
brilliant blue sea,
white caps.
I open the car window wider -
there it is - the breeze, with a
touch of ozone; slightly salty -
what I always remember -
the scent of summer
by the sea.

"Let's walk the beach -
we'll hunt for interesting shells
or polished stones for Mom and Dad,
for pocket pieces."
The older two vie to find
the fanciest shells, the best and
smoothest stones.
Little brother is happy
to investigate the sun-warmed
tidal pools.

A tiny snail, a miniature scallop shell -
fascinating to him.

I stand, looking around,
enjoying the sea, this family day,
holding in my hand the smooth
"feeling stone" just given to me
by my daughter.
I take a deep breath and there it is again -
salt air, a whisker of a tang from
the seaweed scattered about -
and perhaps an overtone of sunscreen
wafted about from those baking themselves
on the sand.
Summer by the sea.

Family days long gone now - and I'm so landlocked -
But on the crest of the Big Green Bridge,
on my way to Maine,
I still reach out my foot
to be the "first one in Maine."
I look eagerly for that first glimpse
of blue water, white caps.
We stop, roll down the windows -
listen to the hiss of the waves,
the rattle of small stones as the waves race.
I inhale - yes, there it is -
I savor once again the salty, briny
scent of summer by the sea -
so deeply planted in my DNA
it forever speaks of home to me.

My younger son lives in the Berkshires-

no casual trips to the sea from there;
but says his best little kid memories
are of blue water, white waves,
and the sound and smell of the sea.

His older brother became at three
a sea lover, we think,
when on his first trip to the shore,
being near a salt marsh (at low tide)
he asked "What is that lovely stink?"
He sees Great Bay each morning
on his way to work;
breathes the sea air
that has become
a part of his early memories.

As for their sister -
she went off to Australia
learned to love the desert,
likes to go bush walking -
but a trip back home
must always include
some days to spend
by the New England Sea.

Light by Dolly Arsenault

The magic of dust motes dancing through a shaft of light didn't lock in my memory until I was four. I remember my small self, sitting cross-legged on the living room rug, transfixed by a rectangular spot of sun coming in the window. I studied the twirling, nearly invisible bits flitting about. Sunshine was magical.

That enchantment never left. When I was several years older, I was taken to Sunday Mass and spent the hour staring at the translucent purples, reds, yellows and blues streaming through stained glass windows.

As a teenager, I'd fill bottles with colored water and place them on an east-facing windowsill. Looking at the rainbow display became a joyful way to begin my day.

In my early twenties, a friend once took me to a museum in Salem to see their exhibit of hundreds of glass flowers. This was nearly fifty years ago, but I never forgot the beauty of so many delicate, glittering pieces. The display soon overwhelmed and I had to leave.

Twenty years ago I bought my condo. From the six units available for sale, I chose one with skylights and an east facing living room window. The sill is wide enough to place two delicate, pink ginger jars; a light, orange bonsai reproduction, and a Josh Simpson planet paperweight. Above the window is a wooden shelf, and dangling from the shelf are three glass baubles, each with different colored swirls. Each morning I sit opposite the window and treat my soul to its daily infusion of light filtering through glass.

And I continue to be charmed by dust motes frolicking in a sun beam.

Fairlight Pool: Sydney by Alice Thomas

royal　　cerulean sea
you wove nodules
of glass and sun
that buoyed my floating eyes

on your sawed shore
lit blue pools
in Australian beads
strung along my poem
on a colorwheel of salty sea
then the sky's thin stairs
darkened   gasped its passage
and all swung open

Three Vignettes on Food and Sustenance by Lori Thatcher

#1 A Lousy Cook

When I was ten, a friend told me her mother had gone back to work and now she got to cook the evening meal. I wasn't jealous. I liked that my mom cooked every meal even though she was a lousy cook.

More cafeteria quality than restaurant fare, certain dishes revisited like unwelcome guests: fish sticks on Friday, tuna macaroni salad on Saturday. American chop-suey stopped in at least twice each week, sometimes—toward the end of the month—with plain ketchup as red sauce. If vegetables accompanied a dish, they were usually either peas or corn.

In lush times, our Sunday plates held boiled dinner made with pork shoulder, white potatoes, cabbage and carrots. I doused the sulfurous cabbage with plenty of sharp-tasting cider vinegar and spread heaps of mustard over the meat and declared it a fine-enough feast.

In lean times, as my mother waited for my tightfisted father to tender the household allowance, we ate a watery sea of potatoes, onions and tiny bits of beef, which my mother christened "Hamburger Soup." To me, it seemed as if "Salty Water

Soup" would have been more fitting.

Even when my father lived with us, the refinement of recipes varied somewhat, but following his hasty move after he was shot in the leg by his mistress's husband, he rarely ate with us and the quality of food deteriorated.

But one thing didn't change. My mother continued to make a big deal of Thanksgiving for us kids. She prepared turkey, turnips, squash, stuffing, and mashed potatoes with smooth golden gravy, along with the ubiquitous peas. She coaxed whole the wine-red cranberry sauce from the can and placed the cylinder intact on a red glass plate next to little bowls of tiny sweet gherkin pickles. Her misshapen apple pie dessert tasted marvelous. Enough leftovers remained for many days of hot turkey sandwiches and root-vegetable mishmashes. Still, I supposed then that anyone could manage a Thanksgiving dinner once a year. I still considered my mother a lousy cook.

Except that label didn't fully define her. When I brought teenage friends home, she deep-fried mashed-potato donuts in a heavy black pot. One after another, delectable, non-greasy pastries emerged from oil heated to the perfect temperature without a thermometer. My friends and I lined up on the other side of the kitchen island waiting for the next one and arguing about who'd already eaten a second. Around the same time, I began to cook certain dishes with one of my vegetarian friends and developed a taste for herbs and spices. My new-found preferences encouraged me to discount my mother's ability even further.

My father was killed in an auto accident six months after my fifteenth birthday, and afterward everything my mother did made me angry. Sometimes I felt as if she disliked me as much as I disdained her.

One afternoon we sat together in silence as Julia Child cooked vichyssoise on the television. I scribbled down the recipe, as I often did, and left the scrap of paper on the end table. The next time my mother shopped, she bought leeks and cream and invited me to help cook the dish. We bumped elbows in the compact kitchen. The broth turned out lumpy, and she whipped the soup smooth with a hand mixer. She and I ate in opposition to each other, me at the small kitchen table and her standing at the counter. I inhaled the complex aroma and sighed. She commented on how such simple ingredients could result in a taste that was so sublime. Then she brought the pot to the table for us to ladle out seconds and smiled at me from across the bowls until I surrendered a grudging smile. And I have never wanted to make vichyssoise since.

Years later, after leaving and returning to that kitchen many times, my husband and I sweated in the driveway as we packed our van to move across the country chasing a California dream. My mother made herself busy in the kitchen. We had stayed with her for several weeks while getting ready and she felt more than unhappy that we were leaving Massachusetts. Every time she and I talked, we ended up arguing. I was already nervous about the move and she sought to make me doubt our decision even further.

As I climbed into the van's front seat, she thrust into my hands a wrapped loaf of still-warm bread scented with toasted onion. It seemed like the blessing that she couldn't speak for a move which took her beloved three-year-old grandson so far away.

We opened the wrapper as soon as we left the driveway and tore off hunks of the loaf—tender-crumbed, fragrant with oat and onion, and delicious. Tears seasoned my piece. I was homesick already for the east coast, for a life that didn't change so fast, and for my mother and her not- so-lousy cooking.

#2. Fried

I met polenta originally in a dismal rest area somewhere in western Pennsylvania, but it was in disguise. At the Amish farmers market, the label identified the cylinder of firm yellow cornmeal as "mush" instead of what I later learned to call it—polenta. I'd never seen such a thing, but it cost only 99 cents, so I bought a package and asked the bearded, straw-hatted seller how to cook it.

"Fry," he said.

At the rest area, I set up a propane camp stove on the picnic table next to our 1963 Econoline van which was piled high with all our belongings. The stove's rusty and partially clogged burner managed only a feeble flame and took forever to heat the cast-iron pan. When the oil finally smoked, I seared thinly-sliced disks of the mush to a golden brown and placed them on paper plates. Slices of scarlet tomatoes and glops of the runny "pot cheese" which the farmer had ladled out of a barrel completed the meal.

The peculiar combination of food and our uncertain circumstances made me queasy. I had never traveled before and felt anxious about our move to the west coast for my husband to attend commercial diving school. We hadn't even arranged where we would live when we got to California, and before we left, my mother warned me, "If you get in trouble when you're so far away no one will be there to help you."

Still, I knew where we'd sleep that night—in the back of our van. Our three-year-old son pronounced the meal "Dee-licious," and my husband smiled at me and squeezed my hand. The first twinge of excitement fluttered in my gut. Our new life might be as different as that polenta had tasted, but everything was going to be okay.

#3. Austrian

"It's good," my mother said, taking another bite of the cake I surprised her with. "But it's not my mother's recipe. She never made this."

Where did I get the recipe written in my own handwriting

on a yellowed and splattered page in the old notebook I used in my high school home economics class? For years I assumed my mother had dictated the recipe to me at some time in the past. Now, she's telling me she has no idea where I got it. Did I copy it from some magazine and it's someone else's "Grandmother's Austrian Plum Cake?"

My grandmother, Agnes Slazak Kurtyka, died when my mother was only eleven. She and my grandfather, Stanislaw, were Austrian immigrants who met in America. After they married and bought a farm in Montague Center, they peddled vegetables, eggs, milk, and butter to surrounding towns.

Their pantry was meager during the depression. My mother told me she remembered her father saying, "We only need a sack of flour and a barrel of sugar and we'll be all right." So I imagined my grandmother saving her pennies and splurging on tiny prune plums and making Austrian plum cake to remind them of their faraway homeland. Except she didn't.

I had made the cake many times, always thinking of it as my grandmother's cake. Now I knew the recipe wasn't hers.

I wondered out loud if I could still consider it my grandmother's cake. My mother said, "I'm sure she wouldn't mind, but I think that it's your cake now."

Strange Leaf by Mildred Grant

First we set up the solar lamp and post as there were several hours of sunlight left in our day to charge the batteries, giving us an outdoor light all night. Otherwise, it would be a very dark night, as there was no moon on the schedule.

Next morning the hurried quarter-mile round-trip to the toilet facility didn't allow for lingering along the way to check the myriad flora and fauna surrounding our campsite.

A vine growing across the road caught my attention. A leaf growing within a larger leaf, how odd a configuration. The center leaf was a smaller, different shape than its host. Upon reaching out (with the idea of picking one leaf set) I found a sharp, unnoticed thorny barrier all along the vine. No samples allowed.

An anemic looking butternut tree was struggling to survive along the south side of our camper. Many pine and hemlock trees, a few balsam and deciduous trees.

Patches of wintergreen and partridge berries dotted the forest floor. Several groups of clintonia, flowers gone by, with blueberries ripening. Evidence of lady slippers in waiting for next spring. Lily-of-the-Valley, bane berry in luscious profusion (poisonous).

So much to see and document, and only ten days to do it all!

"Who Cooks For You Aaalll?" by Noreen O'Brien

Standing at the window under the cover of darkness, I have been eavesdropping on the intimate conversation that is taking place outside my window. I can't help myself. There is no hope that I will ever know what is being discussed between the two Barred Owls, but my guess is that he is whispering sweet nothings into her ear.

'Tis that time of year for these owls—time to select a mate and begin preparations for setting up housekeeping. Too dark to see what is happening out there, I judge from the closeness of the calls and reckon the birds are in the evergreen nearest the dooryard and close to the window. Perhaps they are making use of the roosting box mounted there expressly for them.

I imagine she is standing inside the box. One third heavier than the male, I see her yellow bill slightly raised in a haughtiness, as he attempts to impress her with his whispering. For her eyes only, he is posing, standing straight and tall on a nearby branch, streaked breast puffed up, a feathered leg extended with talons pointing as he shows off the fine tools that he will use to keep her and their offspring well fed as they engage in raising a family in the coming months.

The two large birds, among the most vocal of our owls, are performing a duet of rich hoots and hollers. At times, the birds sound much like monkeys conversing; at other times, they share a rather soft maniacal laugh. Their most common and definitive call is, "Who cooks for you . . . who cooks for you aaallll?" Now, however, they exchange low grunts, and an occasional soft bark or an excited "hoooo-waaah."

Perhaps they have been debating the value of a "previously owned" nest site where a family of Red-tailed Hawks once lived. The male owl likely selected this site in early autumn, and it must now meet with her approval. Among other things, she is looking for a location that has some, but not too dense an understory for protection from predators, as well as a good source of food in the immediate vicinity. A few more minutes of this intimate exchange and all is quiet. Perhaps the pair moved off into the night in the silence of owl flight.

Moments later, I turn on a porch light out back before taking out the dog. Instantly, I see a pair of dark eyes turn toward the light—I have disturbed an owl perched atop the bat house—the birds moved only as far as the backyard. Apparently, this bird is hunting—or I have interrupted some mating ritual—because it remains still, but watching the area of the door.

Within a few moments, unperturbed by the light, the owl drops to the forest floor only to lift up seconds later, long yellowish legs dangling, looking much like the legs of a night heron, talons empty. The bird flies into the darkness beyond the range of the light.

Waiting for the teakettle to boil, I stare out the window into the space where the bird was, feeling awe-inspired over my pre-dawn experience. Then I spot it: a barred owl, looking all superior, perched on a horizontal branch just inside the circle of light. Is it the first owl still hoping to catch the same critter, perhaps in the hopes of impressing its mate, or is it the mate, still waiting to be impressed?

I don't dare reach for binoculars—I am afraid to breathe. I remain still as a rock. Peering out the window, I mentally tick off the key identification points of the grayish-brown Barred Owl: about 20 inches tall, barring on the feathers of the upper breast to the throat, and below that, a pale breast and underparts heavily streaked with dark, elongated markings. Its round, "earless" head has dark eyes—our only owl with brown eyes—within the well-defined facial disc. The bird's head turns first over its right shoulder, then over its left, as it surveys the ground below its perch. What is it hearing that I cannot?

I have moved from eavesdropper to voyeur—and still I cannot stop myself. I know I'll be back tomorrow morning before first light, on the lookout for more intimate exchanges between the Barred Owl pair. It is my hope that they, too, will be back.

In Respect by Sherry Payne Kohler

Jupiter sings through space like the others
And the Painted Turtle still lives by the wood
The orange spot is elliptical to remind
Love awakened to one includes us all
Inheritance a transitory glory lives on

Subject to single acts each by each
This ellipse is not an eye but an island of order
Flowering from leaves of chaos.

The eye of the turtle determines her action
And the sun is warm on her carapace
Through eons she survived without help
And Oh, my own kind: Let it be, Let her be.
Let joy and gratitude join
The celebration of life and the spheres
Where Jupiter swings in his orbit
And Earth on the back of the turtle
Is a dream I live & believe in.

CHAPTER FIVE

Tell Me

Sounds of Blade on Ice by Noreen O'Brien

The first time I tried on a pair of ice skates, though terrified, I was determined to learn to skate. Kathy, Louise, and Mary took turns holding me under my arms, leading me onto the ice amidst the throngs of skaters and hockey players whizzing around us at what I was certain was the speed of light.

My knees were like jelly and my ankles turned inward, looking to meet the ground, resisting what was being asked of them: to support me on the smooth, slippery surface of solid ice while balancing on thin, single blades of metal. No double-runners for me.

Glen Park, a huge ballpark, was two doors down from where I lived. Every winter, the city would build an ice skating rink by dumping dirt mounds around the perimeter of the park, and then flooding the center with a thick layer of frigid rushing water from fire hydrants. The excitement at the sound of that heavy equipment working out there in early November and knowing what was to come still sends the adrenalin up a notch when I think about it. I could barely think of anything else—and I could not sleep—as I waited for the first freeze of winter to solidify the flooded ballfield.

Racing home from school every day so I could get out onto the ice, nothing else mattered to me. Ice skating became an obsession—much as reading was, or as bird watching would become later. I spent hours and hours on that ice, braving the biting wind and stray hockey pucks that caused excruciating pain when they bounced off an ankle. My hands and feet might be bright purple and numb, but I would not—could not—give in to the cold. I had to know how to skate and I had to know it well.

Never was I dressed warm enough. A warm hat? I didn't own one. I wore one of those wide, knitted headbands that run across the top of the head from earlobe to earlobe, like a giant, flattened worm, tied under the chin with lengths of two skinnier worms, full of tight knots I could never get out. My hat was gray with individual silver sparkly circles stitched all over it.

My best friend, Kathy, was beautiful and rich. She wore earmuffs, or a hat similar to mine, but of a much thicker yarn, often a clean, bright white. She had a muffler for her hands, worn over warm, bulky mittens that matched her hat. Kathy wore stretch pants with loops at the cuffs that passed through the skate blades and snapped on the other side of the pant leg, keeping them from riding up and the cold draft from creeping up her legs beginning at the ankles. Sometimes, she wore a skating skirt over these stretch pants. I would have looked silly in such an outfit—it simply was not me.

In time, while I had nothing like Kathy's snug pants or layers of brightly colored bulky sweaters or coverings for my hands, I learned to fly across that ice at least as well as Kathy could. Still, I did have bells on my hand-me-down skates as Kathy wore on hers, mine silver, hers red, blue or green, depending upon her mood and sometimes worn in clusters, one of each color. I guess I looked like something of a ragamuffin. However, when it came to ice-skating, I could not have cared less about my appearance. I wasn't out there for a fashion show—I was there to skate.

More important to me was to be a part of the throng making those lovely scraping sounds of blade on ice. The soft, muffled clunk of metal to diamond-hard ice surface as my foot touched down to propel me forward, faster and faster, my eyes watering from the icy wind. The soft continuous "shhhhh" as my blades rode atop the surface at high speed, and the sound of the swirl as my skates carried me into a reversed direction, making yet another new swish, swish, swish as I created a pair of curvy lines, carved in front of me on the top layer of ice.

I wanted to be on that ice until I died—and would have been happy to be there until that moment came.

Scenes of Glen Park with swarms of kids whizzing by every which way and hockey pucks swishing between players of several hockey games are etched in my brain forever; however, I was barely aware of anyone else out there while I was on that ice. I was oblivious to the backdrop of screams of laughter from those sledding and coasting on the park's hillside, bordering the skating area.

Of course, I also was unaware of the moment the park lights went on at dusk signaling it was time for me to get home. I simply never noticed that moment—I was too busy learning how to twirl, create figure eights, circles, skating on one foot and—what I loved best—skating backward creating those long-distance double-lined curvy paths edged with ice dust. Who needs to eat when the park is flooded? There is always time for food, but the ice will be gone before we know it and the park will then be filled with softball games, foul balls bouncing off the backstop fence and fans in the bleachers screaming insults at the umps.

Am I the only who longs for winter before it is even over?

About 1890 by Mildred Grant

In serious need of a break from his recently established routine, John decided to take the time to search for the pond the real estate agent had assured him was on this property. The agent hadn't seen the pond himself, but had taken the word of the former homeowner that it existed. It was to be reached only by a faint trail up the highest mountain behind the house and barns.

Before leaving the house, John left a brief note for his new bride. "Gone rambling. Back for lunch."

The trail to the pond started from the fence line at the back of the pasture behind the smallest of the three barns.

He and Martha had purchased the farm, land and buildings, over a month ago. John wondered where all the days and nights had gone. Mostly to cleaning and settling into the roomy old house and getting acquainted with their new neighbors, taking no time for really enjoying their surroundings.

Finally, John found the beginning of the trail. Looking up, he wondered whether he would be able to keep his promise to be back here at lunchtime. The mountain looked so very high from down here.

In many places the forest undergrowth was already beginning to take over its rightful domain, leaving John to guess at the next step and direction, slowing his upward progress considerably.

A slight rustling in a large swamp alder to John's right stopped him in his tracks. Monitoring him, through the blossoming branches, stood what looked to be a very large deer.

"Oh, what a beauty!" breathed John.

The deer began to snort and paw the ground before bounding away up the hill into deeper woodland. As John started to step forward to follow the doe, he realized there was something else behind the alder bush. A quick, cautious peek. The doe, by dashing noisily away, had nearly tricked John into following her and missing her precious, new-born fawn nestled in a hollow at the base of the shrub.

Awestruck, John gazed at the baby until he again heard the doe pawing and snorting from further up the trail. John went on with a smile of pure joy wreathing his tired features.

"Not enough smiling, lately. Too much nose to the grindstone stuff," he thought.

As he made his way further up the mountain, John suddenly thought, "I have everything any man could ask for. A beautiful new wife, my dream fulfilled of owning a huge farm with solid buildings, glorious nature at every turn, and even an intriguing mystery pond to explore. Yet here I am, greedily looking for something more."

Going further up the indistinct path, a stealthy movement on an overhanging branch directed John's eyes up into the next tree. Surely he was imagining the long, sleek form that was making the branch quiver? No! Excitement coursed through his veins as the marvelous, sleepy yellow eyes followed his every move.

"Oh, oh, you leave that new baby alone, Mr. Cougar," John admonished. "Such a magnificent beast!" All lithe, rippling muscles, his tail flexed lazily and the dappled sunlight gave his coat a bronzed to light cream appearance.

Through a break in the tree canopy, John realized that same sun indicated the lunch hour was fast approaching. The temptation to go on and reach the pond, right now, was very strong, but his experiences with the doe, fawn, and now the cougar seemed to have satisfied his urge to expand his horizon beyond the immediate needs of getting settled into his new home.

"I've been given this rare preview of the natural bounty of

my land that will live in the back of my mind for total recall, until I can dip into more of the treasures this mountain holds."

As John stood looking up at the cougar, the animal unfolded his huge right leg and fore paw from under his body, letting it dangle just three feet above John's head, as if counseling him to relax and enjoy his surroundings.

"Oh yes, I'll be back, and soon." John vowed, as he turned to retrace his steps. A few feet back down the trail, John glanced back over his shoulder. The cougar was indulging in a huge, potentially jaw breaking yawn that revealed two gleaming, and very lethal looking rows of his offence/defense system.

Turtle by Ted Scott

BANG! The race started. People around me started to push slowly toward the front of the pack. I had positioned myself near the back so I wouldn't interfere with faster runners. I expected to gradually pass runners during the race, since there were always those who started off too fast. But even though I had started near the back, I was surprised at the number of runners passing me in the first couple of minutes. I didn't seem to be passing anyone. I had never come in last in a race before, and the possibility was frightening.

As people continued to pass, the rumble of running shoes on gravel diminished, and a deadly quiet set in. I had been watching the heart rate monitor on my wrist from the beginning. It had moved very rapidly from about 60 to 147 in the first minute of the race, but I didn't feel like I was running fast. I felt fine and like I could go faster, but since 147 was my theoretical peak heart rate, I was afraid to go faster. I knew that if the heart rate went up too much at the beginning of a run, it would suddenly start getting extra beats and jump up to 190 or more, and if I stayed more than a minute or so at such a high rate, I would need to walk or even stop for a few minutes and it would be likely to happen again and again, and I might not be able to finish the race.

In the quiet loneliness of my situation I thought about stopping at the first mile mark and just walking back to the start. Then I saw a very old man just ahead. He was short and stocky and he reminded me of my wife's Italian grandfather when he was 85. He was wearing shorts and plodding steadily along, with his powerful looking legs working like pistons but taking very small steps. I was going quite a bit faster. He must have started near the front. I knew I could pass him and not have to worry about coming in last. But what if he finally gave up and didn't finish? Then I might still be last.

Then an evil thought came to mind. What if I just stayed with him all the way to the finish line? Maybe watchers would think I was just looking out for him and sacrificing my chance for glory. Then at the last minute I could jump ahead and leave him to last place. But he could still quit, and then I would have to quit also, and if I was going to quit, I'd rather do it at mile one than someplace deeper into the race. Just then I saw the last person ahead of me stop beside the gravel road, and before I got there, another woman came back to meet her. This was more like it. I knew I could run at this pace forever. My heart rate was a very steady 147, so I decided to continue the race. I passed the old man and the two women and remained in sight of the tail end of runners about a hundred yards ahead. Once I had passed a few more people, I began to lose my fear of coming in last. I started to enjoy some of the little duels that occurred along the way; like when I sighted a pretty woman with a blond ponytail gradually falling behind the little pack she was with. As she gradually fell further behind, she slowed and began to walk, enabling me to almost catch up with her. Then she sped up again and pulled well ahead of me, but before she could catch her pack she had to slow down again. This time I got a little ahead of her before she sped up again. The same thing happened again and again until finally she couldn't catch me. It reminded me of fishing, how you let the fish go out and then you reel him in a bit and then in and out till the fish finally gives up. I felt like "The Old Man and the Sea."

I had the same experience with a group of two and then a group of three, and the competitive spirit moved me, even in such a strange situation. It was wonderful. I remembered what it had been like once or twice when I was a better runner and at the end of a race I could put on a burst of speed and pass five or ten runners going up the little hill at the end, and listen to the crowd at the finish line cheer. They would always cheer when there was a sprint at the end.

I was using my heart rate monitor to pace myself during the race. Once my heart rate got over about 155, I would slow down enough to get it back in the 145 range. Near the end of the race there were two people ahead that I had been following for perhaps half a mile. I could never seem to make up any yardage on them, but they never pulled further ahead. Like me they were running at a slow but very steady pace. I decided to pass them when we got closer to the finish line. I would run and forget about the heart rate for a little while. I wondered whether either of them would want to challenge me when I went by. I was hoping for a sprint to the finish.

When we were about 200 yards from the finish line, I gradually increased my speed till I passed the woman who'd been 20 yards ahead, then I ran at a steady but increased pace till I caught the man who had been 30 yards ahead. It was about 50 yards to the finish line, and I ran just even with the man, trying to lure him into a sprint for the finish. He refused to go faster so I sprinted alone to the finish. There wasn't a big crowd at the end, but my friends Al and Judy were there and they gave me a big cheer. My heart rate at the finish was 170. I never felt so good at the end of a race.

    At the race today
    Too many rabbits to win
    But he won't be last

Archeology by Alice Thomas

we knit ourselves into a crevice
not reachable
with ax   or sonnet
heavy   impervious
sticky in today's air

if we can/will not move
we wedge   in
everyone else's eternity
then the sandy surfaces
of time   will piece our place

After The Vigil by Ted Scott

    The clock struck noon. We all looked up at the bank clock to confirm; this stint was done. With most of the others, I walked over to the large blue sign-holder bag to replace my sign, a different one from my usual "END THIS WAR" sign. This one had to do with bombs and schools, but I don't remember exactly.

    I'm thinking of making my own sign, as many of the

regulars have. I used to think of myself as an original thinker, at least in the realm of politics, but then I came to see the rationality of Leninism, with the PLP, and then I saw it break up and decline, as the Vietnam War was ending. The only surviving movements have been the "Peacenik" brethren, so that's where I find myself today. Our signs are such a hodgepodge of slogans, taunts, and ideologies that I almost laugh to see us, but I love these people, so innocent, so kind, so cheerful, and life loving.

Several had seen my letter to the Recorder, explaining our vigil as I saw it, responding to Dan Brown and inviting him to visit, acknowledging my role as newcomer. I explained my intent to remove the fear that some may have had of us unfamiliar folk from a scary tradition, protesters, maybe un-American, perhaps dangerous. No – we're just people; people who choose to stand witness for a principle, the principle of peace and justice, and whatever embellishments each sign holder might choose to add.

Next to me, my dear friend Tom, with words at the bottom of his sign "Smash Capitalism," and next to Tom, my newer friend Eric, whose sign said "Pray for Peace." They discussed the word "Smash." Eric offered several alternatives; the most memorable was "Overcome," but there was still no agreement. They have been at it for two years. I still like "smash," but who am I to say, in such a gentle war of words.

I am amazed by Tom. He seems to know everyone, their names, their faces, their life stories, where the live, where they stand (politically). He's so good. He would have made a great communist (Leninist) back in the days when I was. Two or three times every Saturday he'll yell out someone's name, a person walking up the street on the other side, or someone in a car on either side. Often they'll come over. He'll introduce them to me. He'll touch our commonality. I'll feel blessed to meet his friend, but in a few minutes, I may forget their name. Tom's older than I am, but he never forgets anything, and he's there every Saturday, rain, snow, or shine.

Tom calls himself an Anarchist. I ask him what that means. I think of all the blame placed on Anarchists in our history. Always throwing bombs, murdering important people, stirring up riots. That's what we're told, he says; but that's not it at all.

Anarchists are people who love the local way. They believe in communities, not governed from above, people living for, and loving, each other, with no harm sent beyond. It sounds a little like what the Libertarians say, but I think the difference is; we wouldn't let big business run the show.

He told me about a group in Europe, maybe Holland or Norway. They studied resources and sustainability. If fairness and equality were the game, everyone would have just one international flight in their lifetime.

Then suddenly, I remembered the night before; at the Harvard Faculty Club. A 70th birthday for my friend, Larry, editor of *The Journal of Quantitative Spectroscopy and Radiative Transfer*, and head of a group at the Harvard–Smithsonian Center for Astrophysics. The party of 14, mostly physicists, mostly younger, and mostly international, from China, Russia, Vietnam, Serbia, members of his group. Such interesting people, with stories to tell. Larry's wife, a beautiful younger Serbian physicist studying "dirty air" pollution, while Larry's specialty is "clean air," spectroscopy of water molecules, ozone, CO, and CO_2. Four young international researchers whom Marina regards as their "children." She envies Val her four nearby grandchildren.

A young Russian told a story of being at a bar with Larry in a small town near Moscow, when a young man he knew from high school showed up in a police uniform totally drunk. He had gained 50 kg since then and was huge. He asked whether Larry was an "Italiano." "No," Sergei replied, "He's Americano." The huge cop then said, "Americano, I must kill him," and he lunged off the bar stool and fell unconscious on the floor.

Larry introduced me as the one who had convinced him to go to MIT, when I was a freshman and he made a visit at age 15. Later I talked him into going to BU grad school. I recalled a story about our BU grad school physics intramural basketball team. We called ourselves the Psi- Stars. (The Schrodinger wave function is represented by the Greek letter Psi, and Psi with an asterisk after it means the complex conjugate of the wave function. It was an important symbol in Physics.)

Larry was our tallest at 6'4". Because of his height he was our center and had to play against the other teams' centers. One of our games was against the BU football team's intramural basketball team. Their center was Reggie Rucker, who would go on to play 12 years in the NFL as a wide receiver. He was by far the best player we encountered in our season. He was only 6'3" but he could jump 10 feet high and make baskets from anywhere on the floor. We almost gave Larry a medal for holding him to 30 points in the game. Our team made 28 points. I don't remember the final score. Larry was one of the tall guys in our wedding party on May Day 1965.

But when I talked with Tom this morning, about that one international flight per person per lifetime, I realized that the only one at the dinner who met that standard was Val. Even I had several flights to Grand Bahama Island when I worked on Polaris.

Larry is a Francophile, spends a month in Paris every fall as one of his perks and he has made hundreds of international flights in organizing and planning the annual international "Hi Tran" conferences that he runs. He has French cousins who fought the Nazis in the resistance during WWII. I should mention that 40 years ago, Larry was the spitting image of a young Jean-Paul Belmondo. He's still good looking, speaks perfect French and drives a fancy sports car. I haven't seen Jean-Paul lately, but he's still around and maybe looks like Larry will in six or seven years.

I Think That I Shall Never See by Estelle Cade

I think that I shall never see
A pair of shoes made just for me.
A pair of shoes
of softest leather-
with proper heel back,
my small and narrow
foot to tether.

No slip, no slide,
no scuffle nor scrape
just a beautiful shoe,
with perhaps a drape -
across the toe.

Yes, I'd like it in red
if you don't mind.
It never, no never
loses its shine.
I'll wear them to church
and out to tea.
My friends will say
"These are so
just right for thee."

No, I know that I
shall never see
those gorgeous red shoes
made just for me.
Italian leather -

so costly today -
but DSW and Payless
are right on my way.
I will find some red shoes
of that I'm quite sure -
"Almost as good"
Is what my budget says
I must endure.

Sharing by Dolly Arsenault

It's difficult to remember a time when I didn't share. Growing up in a large family, I never considered any possession truly my own. The old adage, "First one up is the best one dressed," was actually true for us. As a child I rummaged through bureau drawers mining for matching socks that would fit. At sixteen I had an after school job which paid enough to buy a few nice clothes. Two of my younger sisters wore my size and for years my meager wardrobe was shared among us three. This seemed normal to us and I can't recall feeling resentment. Happily, by the time I married, my teenaged sisters were working part-time and able to clothe themselves.

Because I believe this was how one lived, I never had a problem sharing in either of my marriages. I note with pleasure that my daughter and daughter-in-law commonly forget who owns what in their household. They divide housework as well as paychecks. I'm delighted they truly act as one, the way a solid marriage should.

With few exceptions, I'm saddened when friends tell me they're estranged from siblings. Often they justify this by stating that they somehow got short changed, whether in parental love or material goods—or sometimes both. I want to shake them and say: "So what! Get over it! Remember—these precious people are the only ones in the universe who share your history and—don't forget—your DNA!

Fluff and quill by Alice Thomas

the fluff and quill of birds leaves me
in awe of their genus and splay
dance rainbows before me as each pre-dawn
call sings of solidarity
large is the purpose of marbled survival
as it falls near my tree
where a molt of truth finds itself in
my pocket of responsibility
actuated - in this time
an autobiography of apart-
ment lives and flies a wildness in the shifting
winds of a birds' contemporary life

Fairy Tales as Truth Tellers by Estelle Cade

Once upon a time there was a little girl
who loved fairy stories.
Not especially the Happily Ever After ones,
but the stories about clever people - or animals -
who turned difficult situations around
and changed them into success stories.

Think about "Puss in Boots"
or "The Three Musicians of Bremen,"
or "The Princess and the Pea."
The little girl grew older, her reading scope widened.
Understood Betsy opened her eyes - use common sense;
Anne of Green Gables, Little Women –
no heroines with easy lives;
they would find strength within themselves to
become themselves,
while still loving others.
What did adulthood teach this little girl?
What life lessons had she garnered?
Perhaps it was that life is not a fairy tale,
but that some of the best life lessons
are taught by fairy tales -
if you know which ones to attend to.
Use your wits; don't be led astray by false promises;
be truthful, be kind;
treat others as you'd want to be treated.
There is no pot of gold at the end of the rainbow;
don't depend on others to make you happy -
that must come from within yourself.
And that "Handsome Prince"?
Don't count on him!

Keepsakes by Janice Lepore

I braced myself against the cold wind and hurried to the house. Shucking my boots, I thought, "This writing assignment is going to be easy." But parading around the first floor in my heavy socks, I wasn't fascinated by any of the furniture or the decorations, which included a beat up piano that I dearly love but seldom play. It had been brought into the house only as far as the back entrance (mud room) and then had transformed into just a place to put stuff—and more stuff.

It was going to be a busy week with doctors and dentists, as well as a full house weekend with grandchildren, so I had vowed to do my homework early, but here it was Monday morning with nothing in black and white. Now it didn't seem as easy as I had anticipated.

There was history connected with certain pieces of furniture and many of the wall pieces had come gift-wrapped. I enjoyed collecting unique photo frames, candlesticks, bookends, letter openers, and bells through the years, especially as mementos of trips here and there. The bell collection had started as pewter, or at least unbreakable materials, but it had expanded to other types and had now reached the point of "no more room". Most of the gift bells were breakable, many representing holidays, and now the collection needed a showcase of its own. Our home is a playhouse for little girls so any glass front cabinet would have to wait.

The second floor survey yielded more clutter—cedar chests and holiday throws and handmade afghans with more history. A collection of books designed to expand my writing capabilities that the girls had rearranged—spine side in—in the bookcase over the weekend, would not be a worthwhile keepsake. It seems I have an affection for paintings, scrapook items, and colorful files that were meant to organize my keepsakes and my writings. Drawers of jewelry waited for display at some tag sale, along with children's toys and puzzles.

Fortunately, my profound inspection materialized an old photo of the current Big H family reunion farm and a 1990 five generation photo including my dad, his uncle, my daughter, her two sons and myself. Now that I had gotten my hands out of my pockets, it was time to admit, in writing, that memories are my keepsakes of the heart to be shared and that's what we try to do in writing class.

My Famous Cousin by Marty Glaser

I didn't find out about my famous cousin until after my parents went to Israel. They spent some months there and then flew on to Los Angeles to visit my brother Jerry and his wife Nan, and their children.

While my parents were in Israel, they attended a dinner party in Tel Aviv and met our cousin, Dan. While at the party, the phone rang and the caller asked for our cousin. What we didn't know was that he was told a hundred Israeli citizens had been kidnapped by PLO terrorists and flown to Uganda.

Dan undertook to extricate himself from a conversation with my mother who had just met him and had many questions. Dan said he had to leave immediately and that it was very important. My mother, usually a better interrogator than the CIA or Mossad in getting information out of everyone, got zero from Dan. She pleaded with him, and said that she and my father had come to Israel specifically to see him, and that they might never be able to come to Israel again. But attempting to lay Jewish guilt on him didn't cut any slack with Dan. He apologized profusely and then left.

The radio and TV carried news about the kidnapping of the Israelis and the demands of the terrorists that Israel release fifty-three Palestinian prisoners within twenty-four hours of the kidnapping or the terminal would be blown up.

Plans were developed to keep negotiations ongoing while the Israeli Knesset and the Israeli Defense Force planned a surgical military incursion. It was fortunate that the construction of the terminal was carried out by an Israeli company, Solel Boneh. In a cooperative venture between Uganda and Israel intelligence, floor plans and runway info were well used by the IDF to save the kidnapped Israelis.

My parents spent the rest of the couple of months visiting other Israeli relatives. After six months, they were at LAX waiting to fly back home to Athol, Ma. While waiting for their flight, they shopped at a book store at the airport. My father leafed through a book called Raid on Entebbe and came to a picture he recognized. He turned to my mother and asked her, "Isn't that your Cousin, Dan?"

They were surprised. In the book, American cousins, without any names stated, who came to visit with Dan and his family were mentioned, along with my mother's pleading with him to stay.

Dan was none other than the Lt. General Daniel Shomron, Chief of Staff of the Israeli Defense Force, who planned and led the daring military operation at Entebbe, Uganda.

Years later, When Lenore and I traveled to Israel, I wanted to look him up and visit him as the son of Dr. Sam and Florence Glaser, his cousin. However, things didn't work out because of lack of time and travel commitments.

On arriving home, I went on to the Internet to look him up. I was overcome with sadness to find that Daniel Shomron had passed away after a heart attack. He was, according to the IDF and the Knesset, the greatest and most decorated Paratroop Commander in Israeli history. Dan Shomron was a soldier who embodied the strength and adaptability of the Israeli Army.

This was my famous cousin, Dan.

Our Old Barn by Janet Keyes

Our barn had a great history. Reportedly it was once the barn behind the large white building at the corner of Main and High Streets next to the Walker Funeral Home. Many years ago, probably before 1910, it was moved all the way to its current location at the end of Colorado Avenue. To move it the new owner (probably Bruno Hartmann) had to dismantle it completely, then move it board by board and beam by beam on horse-drawn wagons. The old construction involved pegs in addition to nails. The round wooden pegs and the old-fashioned cut nails were carefully removed, then re-used at the new location. I'm not sure what the wood was. Chestnut was the most common old wood, but this was likely something else.

Bruno Hartmann had a small farm, maybe 70 acres, and he kept a few cows and sold milk to his neighbors in that small German community. The barn was about 30 by 30 with two large lofts connected by a smaller loft at the front of the building. The barn had to accommodate two or three cows, two draft horses, and lots of hay in addition to a small space for grain, tack, and tools.

Bruno and his brothers, the chemist and the machinist (Rob and Max), owned the property a long time. During World War I they were informally restricted to the farm because of their alleged admiration for the Kaiser. A kind gentleman named Alphonse Patnode would go into town and buy groceries and other necessities for the family, which included a sister Anna. Neighbors would come to the farm to get their milk. Down on the hillside there were a couple of small buildings which were probably chicken coops. I assume at least one of those belonged to the Hartmanns, as it was falling into extreme disrepair by 1960. The Hartmanns went back to Germany after the war, and gave the farm to Mr. Patnode in thanks for his kindness.

The barn has stood sturdy and strong for many years. When I first knew it, there was an old "office" room at the front, with many prize ribbons left there by a horse owner, George Patnode. There were two large box stalls with half-doors scarred along the top by the "cribbing" of the draft horses. (Bored horses chew the wood on their doors.) The walk-through door leading into the office still worked. The lofts were being used as storage space for old furniture, an old ice sled, some scrap lumber, and more obscure treasures.

Over the years the barn has leaned a little to the east. At one time we jacked it up and added bracing to reinforce the strength of the building. Now when it tries to lean, it actually tightens the bracing and becomes stronger. We even got the walk-through door working again. Then in more recent years we got busy. Allan had some health problems, and we built a house on the other side of town. The barn started leaning aggressively to the east, pushing the walk-door into the ground. The west end of the barn started to buckle a little, and panes of glass have popped out of the windows on the south side of the barn. Occasionally a slate from the roof falls off, and Allan slides a piece of metal roofing into the space. Squirrels like the way the trees north of the barn have grown larger and longer branches, making it easy to include the barn in their daily route. Squirrels are bad for buildings, and we have seen larger and newer chewed-out holes they have created to improve their traffic flow. An expert tells us our barn could still be jacked and saved, but we are not there to use it.

We have been trying to sell the place on and off for several years, and we realize the barn's deteriorating condition seriously detracts from what realtors call "curb appeal." Last year we talked with a man who will take the barn down in exchange for the salvaged materials. Old barn boards have value even if they aren't gray. Varying shades of worn and faded red are also desirable.

Late in the fall he told us he had not forgotten us and would see us in the spring. Spring came very late and now the man is putting on an addition to our daughter's home so her mother-in-law can move in with them. I guess we're not the only procrastinators who overbook our time.

Two years ago we removed a lot of stuff from the lofts. Allan's Red Ryder BB gun was there, to his surprise. His oldest bike had been stolen. Our cellar now has the double-rip sled, the ice sled, several chairs in need of re-building, and boxes of old tools and glassware. We gave a lot of old metal stuff to my nephew to sell for scrap. Allan still wants to remove the horse stall doors to use again, perhaps in the cheap new barn we hope to build behind our new home. We have fond memories of the horses we kept in that barn, but Allan likes his memories reinforced with souvenirs.

Our computer still stores the last good photo of the barn, taken when the barn looked presentable. The barn appears as a dark red shadow, softened and framed in falling snow. I'll enjoy remembering it that way.

Ravens Sent From Heaven by David Allen Bryant

Some years ago I was ill with the flu. I got very thin and had pain in my heart, dizzy spells and everything else that goes along with the flu. I thought that I had an especially bad case because I had gotten a flu shot after I already had the flu.

One day I had to go out even though I was still ill. As I started to get into my car, I saw hundreds of huge jet-black birds sitting on the roof top of the building where I lived. They surrounded me, perched on fences and trees. People who passed took notice.

What troubled me most was that they were sitting there intently, looking as if they were concerned. I instinctively knew they were concerned about me.

To see this great number of birds seemed Divine as well as majestic. I was so ill, I really believed that I was going to die. Then I remembered that it was God that sent them there to remind me that he is there. Everyone who witnessed the birds was amazed. I could see it by the expressions on their faces.

It was the love and Almighty Hand of Jehovah and I will never forget that day.

I recovered very quickly after that and I am convinced it was because God intervened in my life.

Grey Cat by Sherry Payne Kohler

You are a shadow at once
Upon my windowsill,
Behind my eyelids
As I love you
And deny you.

But how full your lighted eyes,
Pale yellows that entreat
And would command.
That wildly ask
"I want."

Epilogue

Now through our window

It is I who look.
Then out into shadows
I go in vain to search
For yellow light.

Had I loved you perfectly
I could have held you
As you died.

Memories of Millie Grant

Janet Keyes

Millie had the most charming way of making us feel we were almost a part of her family and a part of her childhood adventures. Who could forget four little children running away from home, and being so kindly rescued by the family doctor? What fun they and we had the day Millie's big brother decided they needed a pet, and enlisted the aid of his little sisters in bringing home a baby skunk the day their mother had her only-ever garden party! Millie gradually and gently introduced us to hints of a less-than-perfectly-joyful life story. I sincerely hope her family will publish all of her stories. Her unique voice shines through all her writings. Most of all I treasure memories of her wit and wisdom, and her friendship.

Dolly Arsenault

I met Millie about five years ago when I first joined the Well Done Writers. My first impression was: how elegant. Her hair was always beautifully styled, her clothes colorful and set off by sparkling jewels; but most striking were her glistening fingernails. I wouldn't be surprised if she'd done her own manicure because everything Millie set her lovely hands to, she did well. She had an amazing voice, decorated beautifully, gave gourmet cooking lessons and knit and sewed. Her vast store of general knowledge was boggling. That she was also an exquisite writer came as no surprise. Millie will be much missed.

Alice Thomas.

Millie Memories: I remember her bluest eyes, caught by the azure sparkle in every facet of the many pins she wore upon her breast. Millie was the quintessential "Lady of Western Mass"; a memory unto herself when exacting a fragment of memoir. She will always be remembered.

Ted Scott

Millie was the most remarkable writer I have ever known. At 94, she could pick up her pencil and pad and write out a true story, with all the dialogue, of some interesting event of her early life. You got to know the characters (her family and friends) almost as well as if you had been there. Likewise, she could bring in a ghost story or other fiction and read it so that you thought it was true, until the surprise ending. I asked her once how long she had been writing and she said "a few years." She was gifted in many other ways: singing, all kinds of crafts, and teaching. She was an inspiration to us all.

Janice Lepore
Remembering Mildred Grant: Millie fascinated me when she read tales of the by-gone years and her siblings and stories of children growing up with ideas of their own. Her descriptions of their home and country area were so comfortable to us as we listened to this active lady in her aging years. If only we could have her interests and abilities to participate so fully in our own last days. We miss you, Millie.

Cathey Boschen
The last time I saw Millie in our writer's group, she commented on how she really connected with the written piece I'd read to the group. Millie was like that, encouraging and supportive. As a newer member of the group, I remember her warm, welcoming greeting as I entered the room. She was always dressed meticulously in color coordinated outfits that reminded me of my mother. She usually came to group with her stenographer's notebook with handwritten stories. The writing would be on the lines and in the margins so she often had to turn that notebook around to read what she'd written in it. She spoke her mind and her narratives were full of rich, colorful details and dialogue that described the many people and events in her life. Millie had a feisty side and I particularly enjoyed listening to her when she spoke about something she was passionate about, especially the new senior center. All of us will greatly miss her.

Marty Glaser
I was new to the Well Done Writers Group and nervous because I wasn't sure I could write well. I met Millie Grant after one session and told her that the writers seemed fantastic and I was just learning. She told me to relax, listen to what everyone read and then use my own unique perspective. So I listened, relaxed and took her advice, which was the best advice I have ever been given about writing. I was mesmerized when Millie read her warm, loving, descriptions of growing up in the area. I could close my eyes and picture the scenes she was describing. When she described a flower, she was so knowledgeable I could almost smell the perfume. When she told stories about her brother always getting into trouble, I could identify with her brother. When Millie read her stories in her soft voice I liked them instantly because they were of real people and the things kids got into. Millie was special to me. Her writing was straight forward, not sappy, yet you could feel the love when she recalled her youth, parents, cousins and grandparents. Millie's writings will always be as real to me as if she were still writing with us. If I ever put together all my writings, I would like to dedicate them in memory of Millie Grant and the Well Done Writers.

Lori Thatcher
What can I say about the Grande dame of the Greenfield Senior Center writing group? Millie astounded me. She had an elegance and softness that concealed true grit. She loved writing—really loved it—and she knew what she wanted to write and how she wanted to write it. And she did it so well. Millie brought stories alive, put you

in the path of a careening carriage or alongside her beloved brother running from a swarm of maddened bees. Her mother's words rang through the room powerfully, even in Millie's quiet voice. On a personal note, each time she walked into the room, she had a way of making me feel she was delighted to see me. I'm quite sure she made each and every one of us feel the same. I will miss her. We will all miss her.

About the Authors

Luci Adams is a Vietnam era veteran, and went to GCC when she got out. She worked for Polaroid for 19 years and came back to the Pioneer Valley in 2006 to look for work. Luci decided she liked not being employed full time, so she retired in February of 2007. Luci enjoys volunteering at her many "jobs" and getting together with friends. Because of circumstances, she is not writing as much as she was, but hopes to do more in the near future.

Dolly Arsenault was born in Lynn and moved in 1971 to western Massachusetts when her husband was accepted at UMA as a Ph.D. candidate. They raised their only child in Greenfield, and Dolly is pleased to say that after college in Boston, she returned to her roots. Dolly worked as a secretary for a non-profit child protection agency for 18 years and retired in 2007. Since then, she has done what she promised herself she would do: write. She was wise enough to join with other writers at the Greenfield Senior Center, and their support and suggestions have been invaluable. She has had pieces published in the collections *Tales and Treasures,* and *Days and Moments, Moments and Days.*

Ellen Blanchette is an artist and writer currently living in Greenfield, Massachusetts. She grew up in Philadelphia, where her mother was a school teacher and a classically trained pianist. Her father was a manufacturer of women's coats with a factory in Camden, New Jersey. Ellen's parents divorced when she was very young, and her mother remarried soon after that. Her half-brother Gordon was her best friend growing up. Ellen attended Overbrook High School in West Philadelphia where music was her main interest. After a time at the Philadelphia College of Art, she moved to New York City where she lived and worked for most of her adult life. She married Joseph

Blanchette in 1968 and their son Paul was born in 1970. Ellen returned to college, studying liberal arts at the City University of New York. She completed a Bachelor of Science Degree in Art and Education in 1977, and a Masters Degree in Creative Writing in 1984, both at Brooklyn College. She and her husband divorced in 1977, after which she raised her son as a single parent in Brooklyn. Ellen moved to Franklin County in 2002, intending to retire, but found herself drawn to contributing to the community in a variety of ways. Ellen has worked as a reporter and photographer mostly at The Montague Reporter since 2008, covering the Gill-Montague school district and writing many feature stories and reviews of theater and arts events. She has also belonged to several local choral groups and has shown her photography in many public art spaces. She finds keeping herself engaged and active makes life a lot more worthwhile.

David Bryant is one of seven children. He was born in Springfield and grew up in New Jersey with two of his brothers. He has two sisters he has not seen since childhood. David loves writing with the others. His strong faith directs his life and comes through in many of his pieces. He has had pieces published many places as well as in the collections: *Tales and Treasures,* and *Days and Moments, Moments and Days.*

Estelle Cade moved to Ashfield from the Boston area at the age of eleven and has been happily settled in Franklin County ever since, although she has traveled quite extensively. Widowed many years ago, she is the mother of three, grandmother of five and great-grandmother of four. Having always been a writer, (she liked writing assignments in school!) she takes great joy in her writing group friends as they share their life stories with each other. She hopes someday her "grands" and "great grands" will enjoy reading the stories of her life in the olden days. She has had work published in all ten volumes of *Local Color, As You Write it Vol. I and II, Tales and Treasures, The Good Life, The Recorder, The Springfield Union, The Ashfield News* and *The Montague Reporter* as well as in the collection *Days and Moments, Moments and Days.*

Marty Glaser was born in Springfield, raised in Athol, and schooled at Worcester Academy, BU College of Basic Studies, Emerson College and Fitchburg State College. He was a Special Education Teacher for forty years, thirty years at the Franklin County Technical School. Marty and his wife Lenore have lived in Turners Falls since 1978 and celebrated their forty-second anniversary on August 18, 2016. They have two grown sons, each having one daughter. Marty joined the Well Done Writers because a *Book of Errors* was in his thoughts. He and Lenore also wanted to create a legacy book for their sons. Marty sees life in humorous ways and says he has grown as a writer because of association with good writers, encouragement to find his own voice, and because of positive suggestions for improving his writing. He enjoys the writing group because they listen, give positive feedback, and respect each other for their unique contributions.

Esther Johnson is a Swede/Finn by heritage and an American by birth. She learned Swedish by full immersion when she was 13 by spending the summer on a farm in Sweden and reading comic books in Swedish called Kalle Anka (Donald Duck). She also talked with her 60-year-old aunt and her family. She has spent over one year in Sweden and speaks, reads and writes the language. Her heritage has made her who she is today. Esther married a second generation Swedish/American, and tried to pass her strong heritage to their children and grandchildren. Esther's love of writing was nurtured by writing newsletters for Scandinavian groups and creating much of the text which led to drafting company newsletters for legal firms and manufacturing enterprises.

Janet Keyes was born in Vermont, and has lived most of her life in Greenfield, ever cherishing the depth of her family roots in Massachusetts. A retired registered nurse, her volunteer work includes Baystate Franklin Medical Center, Greenfield Senior Center, and Robbins Memorial Congregational Church. Janet's literary interests date back to the Bookworm Club in her childhood, then her position on the staff of her high school newspaper, and years of work on church newsletters. Currently she is group leader of the Well Done Writers. Over the years, her poems and essays have been published in the *Greenfield Recorder*, *Local Color*, *The National Library of Poetry*, *Senior News*, and the writing group publication, *Tales and Treasures*, as well as in the collection *Days and Moments, Moments and Days*. She sings in her church choir and has composed lyrics for several hymns. She enjoys sharing slip-of-the-tongue "geezerisms" with her husband Allan who has also collaborated with her in writing stories of family history.

Sherry Payne Kohler, A Bio' 2016
A Thinker more than doer
A Skeptic more than believer
- And somewhere in between.
A Lover of truth, and the myriad
Forms of beauty; the animate
The inanimate - and all the inbetweens.

Janice Lepore, a retired secretary, mother of four and grandmother of seven, was born and raised in South Dakota. She was the eldest of fourteen. Her work has been published in *The International Library of Poetry*, *Greenfield Senior News*, *The Good Life*, and *Local Color* as well as in the collections *Tales and Treasures, and Days and Moments, Moments and Days*.

Noreen O'Brien has been chasing winged, feathered creatures for some 45 years and, at every opportunity, has traveled the globe with birds as the focus of each trip. In addition to birds, Noreen has enjoyed a lifelong passion for reading, journaling, and will sometimes delve into the world of writing creative nonfiction and memoir—she reads and writes to discover what she thinks and feels about things.

Lettice Randall, had in the past, lived in Greenfield and attended the Well Done Writers group there at the Greenfield Senior Center. In 2014 she returned to her hometown of Shelburne Falls after the death of her husband, Charlie. She has since then been attending a writing group at the Shelburne Falls Senior Center. She hopes to get back to more writing and also hopes to do some freelance verse writing for greeting card companies as she had in the past for the Oatmeal Studios, a greeting card company based in Rochester, VT. In 1996 she won the Oatmeal Studios most Creative Editorial award for one of her contributions. In 2010 Lettice had pieces in *Tales and Treasures* and in the 2014 collection *Days and Moments, Moments and Days*. In her free time, Lettice enjoys the company of her three children all of whom live locally, and her five grandchildren and one great-grandchild.

Ted Scott moved to Greenfield in 2006 after teaching Physics for over 30 years. He began writing by taking memoir writing classes at GCC and has been part of a writing group since then. He occasionally reads at local "Open Mic" groups, and has been attending the Greenfield Senior Center Writing Group since 2009. His latest publication (Fall 2013) was "US Out of Vietnam!" a memoir piece in THE VETERAN a semiannual publication of the Vietnam Veterans Against the War. Ted is 79 but is not a veteran.

Lori Thatcher is a writer, editor, and collector of stories. She joined the Greenfield Senior Center writing group in the spring of 2011 and developed the group's website, WellDoneWriters.com shortly after. She mainly writes short forms of memoir and short fiction, and has had two stories published in anthologies, one chosen for one of the featured author's pick in the anthology, *It's a Crime*. She enjoys working with senior writing groups and offering prompts to motivate seniors to share their stories. For a time before she moved to Maine, she was one of the leaders of The Well Done Writers. In 2014 she edited and published a collection of their stories: *Days & Moments, Moments and Days* - a senior anthology.

Alice Thomas is a poet, news-feature writer, photographer, videographer, and artist who is published on-line, in anthologies and news articles. Her art exhibitions are accompanied by her poetry in the genre of ecological topics.